I'm not afraid to ____ the chef
confront ?

- Fair
- Consistent
- Equitable

Not an Outsider, I'm within
the community.

Henderson + Henderson → Research

MY FATHER'S
Faith

LaNeesha,

All my best!

[signature]

4/29/16

MY FATHER'S *Faith*

DR. JACQUELINE M. GAITHER RESPRESS

MY FATHER'S FAITH

Copyright © 2015 Dr. Jacqueline M. Gaither Respress, BS, EdM, EdD.

All rights reserved. No part of this book may be used or reproduced by any means, graphic, electronic, or mechanical, including photocopying, recording, taping or by any information storage retrieval system without the written permission of the author except in the case of brief quotations embodied in critical articles and reviews.

Editors:
Michele McBurney
Akilah E. Daniels

iUniverse books may be ordered through booksellers or by contacting:

iUniverse
1663 Liberty Drive
Bloomington, IN 47403
www.iuniverse.com
1-800-Authors (1-800-288-4677)

Because of the dynamic nature of the Internet, any web addresses or links contained in this book may have changed since publication and may no longer be valid. The views expressed in this work are solely those of the author and do not necessarily reflect the views of the publisher, and the publisher hereby disclaims any responsibility for them.

Any people depicted in stock imagery provided by Thinkstock are models, and such images are being used for illustrative purposes only. Certain stock imagery © Thinkstock.

ISBN: 978-1-4917-7792-3 (sc)
ISBN: 978-1-4917-7791-6 (e)

Library of Congress Control Number: 2015917052

Print information available on the last page.

iUniverse rev. date: 11/16/2015

To the memory of my parents, Rev. Israel Lee and Lillian Johnson Gaither. Thank you for your faith, wisdom, inspiration, and prayers. Without your guidance, I would have wavered.

Rev. Israel Gaither, 1940

Rev. Israel Gaither, 1993

Contents

Introduction xi
Chapter 1: The Foundations of My Faith 1
Chapter 2: A Synopsis of My Father and My Family 8
Chapter 3: Memories from the Past 30
Chapter 4: A Few of the Miracles in My Life 34
Chapter 5: The Influence of Spirituality and Faith on Educational Research 41
Chapter 6: The Growing of My Faith 50
Chapter 7: The Benefits of Being Faithful 57
Chapter 8: The Stories You May Not Believe 75
Chapter 9: My Educational Philosophy 87
Chapter 10: The Conclusion of the Matter 101
Epilogue 109
References 113
About the Author 117

Introduction

The day started as uneventful, just like most other wintery mornings in eastern Ohio, except I neglected to view the news and weather forecast on the local television station while dressing. The air was crisp and dry when I began my thirty-minute commute to work. As time passed, I heard talk of an impending storm from my fellow teachers but prayed it would simply pass over. At every opportunity I glanced outside the window, hoping my fears were not justified.

Just after lunch the announcements began for the early dismissal of one school district after another. A sick feeling was housed in the pit of my stomach as I anticipated the treacherous ride home. My head began to ache when I realized I didn't even have the simplest of tools readily available to remove mounting snowdrifts from my car.

I had inadvertently forgotten to transfer a snow brush from my kitchen to my car. I would be forced to remove the five or so inches of snow by hand, without even the benefit of gloves. I hesitantly walked toward the exit, mad at the blizzard and myself. Then I spotted him.

My father was next to my car, sweeping snow from the windows and body of the vehicle on the icy parking lot, working away without hesitation. He had already dug out the area around the car and put ashes near the tires. He smiled as I approached, and I thanked him profusely for his assistance. Something in his smile always gave me peace. He inquired about my day and encouraged me to spend the night at his house rather than risk an accident.

Extra clothes were always at my parents' house, and I knew he would drive me to school the next day, if necessary. Once the removal was complete, he left to clear another car at another school to ensure that my sister would be safe.

Years earlier my father had accompanied me to a conference regarding a teaching position. I overheard the interviewer jokingly refer to him as my bodyguard. If that was what he needed to be, that was the role in which he served. That was the kind of father he was, always there when one needed him. I came to depend on him when trouble was on the horizon or when I could simply use a word of encouragement. I believed that his prayers were more powerful than my own and that he could touch the throne of glory with ease. He stood up for his children and raised us to be proud of our heritage. He defended and protected us for as long as he had the breath to do so. His strong Christian virtues as a man and father are the premise for this writing.

Anyone can record his or her life's story for the sake of writing. Biographers have been known to dredge up memories that might have been better left forgotten. Other authors dig deep into their souls and find something meaningful to impart that gives insight into present, past, or future difficulties. At my retirement party as principal of the New Castle Junior/Senior High School, I received a gift from a friend, an unlined journal.

She said, "Now write the book."

I procrastinated for three years. So many conversations ran through my mind. Numerous experiences in my life and educational career made it difficult for me to decide what to tell and what not to tell. There were also those stories that nobody would believe if I told them. Although honesty was my best policy, I did not want to offend anyone who might recognize him- or herself in my storytelling. Still I had a compelling duty to remain true to my own convictions.

This work has also allowed me to review and adjust my thinking, to some extent. As I reflected on the past, I recognized that persons who had offended me were held in high esteem by others at the same time.

A measure of peace emanates from me as I examine the course of my life walk and share it with people along the way. I am convinced that all we enjoy and endure have been sifted into the making of more perfected beings.

I have told the stories in narrative form. I didn't want to change the names of those involved in order to "protect the innocent," so many have not been identified, or they have sometimes been referred to in unrecognizable terms. I am mindful that these experiences are viewed through the lenses of my own eyes. Therefore my feelings are exposed in the text but in the most objective format at my disposal. All the positive and negative events have ultimately worked together for my good and provided the core of my personal testimony.

I believe, however, that faith goes far beyond the borders of my being and thinking. I have included educational research on spirituality and faith to validate the academic philosophies that I have come to acquire. Other opinions are my own.

This book is entitled *My Father's Faith* because of the profound effect that my late father, the Reverend Israel Lee Gaither II (May 18, 1913–January 31, 1996), had on my life. He was a loving father, a hardworking husband, an exceptional singer and preacher, a long-suffering pastor, and an excellent model for those who wanted to walk in the Christian faith. His eighty-three years on this earth should not go unnoticed. His legacy continues to live on. I trust that these few passages give a glimpse of the man I loved and admired.

Chapter 1:
THE FOUNDATIONS OF MY FAITH

But without faith it is impossible to please God.
—Hebrews 11:6

On countless occasions I have contemplated the impact of faith and spirituality on my life. As a child I acquired an unpretentious definition of faith by using the acronym FAITH (for all I trust Him). Faith goes much further than that simplicity.

Merriam-Webster provides a formal definition of *faith* as "a strong belief or trust in someone or something; belief in the existence of God; strong religious feelings or beliefs or a system of religious beliefs." It occurs when a person places his or her total confidence in, and acknowledges unreserved dependence on, God. Faith is normally embedded within the sphere of traditional doctrines and religions. The faith I have does not rely on proof; it is based on expectations.

This faith I speak of rests on the assurance that God will provide for all my needs according to His riches in heaven. He does indeed take care of me. The Epistle of Paul to the Hebrews defines *faith* as "the substance of things hoped for, the evidence of things not seen" (Heb. 11:1). Other scriptures clarify faith as a source of healing (Matt. 9:2); a means of protection from the wicked (Eph. 6:16); a manual for living (Hab. 2:4);

an aid in developing patience (James 1:3); and an encouragement for believers to stand firm and be strong (1 Cor. 16:13).

My hero, my father, the late Reverend Israel L. Gaither, who displayed his confidence in God until the day he died, instilled in me at a young age the notion of depending on my heavenly Father.

In the secular world, men and women easily accept occurrences as presented. When we turn our car keys, we expect the engines to roll over and start up so we can reach our destinations. By flipping a light switch, darkness disappears, and the room is illuminated.

Our unconscious faith reflects itself in the plans we make for future vacations and adventures, not considering the fact that death is only a heartbeat away. Truthfully we begin to die the day we are born. There are short graves as well as long graves in the cemetery because death is no respecter of persons. We have faith that when we sit on benches, they will hold our weight and not give out. This type of gratuitous faith goes without saying or thinking. Why, then, is it so difficult to garner faith in God?

This is a record of one woman's journey guided by faith.

You may ask, "Why did you choose to disclose an account of your life?" Or you might even inquire, "Why should I care to read it?"

You can only find that answer within your heart as you peruse my chronicle and scrutinize the tragedies and difficulties I have faced. I request only that you embrace the story. I do not intend for the words of this text to be a manual for women only; nor are they to be regarded simply as an African American's tale of woe. I aim to share my experiences and perspective of my walk with God.

Do not feel sorry for me because of the hindrances I have encountered. My tests, you see, are the basis of my testimony. If we had no problems, we could not fathom that God could solve them. If we had no complexities, we would not realize His ability to make sense of the complications. If there were no mountains blocking our way, we would not muster the stamina to climb them or have the voice to tell them to get out of the way. I am convinced that the situations in my life bolstered my dependence on my heavenly Father.

Jesus said unto His disciples, "Have faith in God. For verily I say unto you, That whosoever shall say unto this mountain, Be thou removed, and be thou cast into the sea; and shall not doubt in his heart, but shall believe that those things which he saith shall come to pass; he shall have whatsoever he saith" (Mark 11:22–23).

To some extent I will explore the plight of the African American female in the United States from both an educational and economic standpoint. I contend that spirituality and faith are significant influences in the lives of African Americans in general, African American females in particular, and Christians inclusively. The combination of spirituality and faith allows people of color to rise above the nuisances of society.

Stewart (1997, 16) writes, "Black people could not have survived without it in a world that continually tried to destroy their personhood, power, and inherent self-worth." He further maintains that the spirituality of African Americans has "enabled them to interpret, confront, embrace, transcend, and ultimately transform the culture of the oppressors into a meaningful reality of soul survivors" (133).

After reading this account, there may be a newfound empathy for the African American female's struggle in America. *My Father's Faith* provides another avenue for Christians to be overcomers and affords a means of empowerment for spiritual maturity.

I have come to believe Jude 1:24–25 with more confidence. "Now unto Him that is able to keep you from falling, and to present you faultless before the presence of His glory with exceeding joy. To the only wise God our Savior, be glory and majesty, dominion and power, both now and ever. Amen."

My Father's Faith is a blend of personal narratives and memories, research on education and spirituality, quotes, and scriptures. I have framed the stories through my eyes. Stories are powerful tools, according to Merriam (2002, 286), and "a basic communicative and meaning-making device pervasive in human experience." They are a persuasive means of communication.

The accounts may at times make you laugh and occasionally bring a tear to your eyes. They depict a lived experience. Perhaps one will be inspired to go further, reach higher, ignore the naysayers, and truly trust God for everything. If you do not or did not have a strong and spiritual earthly father to nurture and teach you as I did, remember that your heavenly Father loves you, cares for you, and desires nothing but the best for you.

You don't have to fall! Learn from the wisdom I have accumulated. A good mother wants her children to avoid the pitfalls of life. Mothers do not want to see any of their kids undergo any pain or strife. If possible, I would ensure that my children never got sick, stumbled and fell, chipped a tooth or skinned a knee, faced discrimination, got overlooked for a promotion, or had their feelings hurt.

In short I would try to give them a perfect existence. That, of course, is an impossible undertaking. I sincerely hope that my sons and daughter have a better life than my own. A good mother cherishes, shields, and provides for her young. We train our toddlers not to touch a stove because they will get burnt. We convince our offspring to gain an education so they can succeed in life. We expose our young ones to cultural events so they will have an expanded knowledge base.

That means our children must set goals early in life. Benjamin E. Mays (Howe 2003, 236) quoted Marian Wright Edelman in the *New York Times* in stating, "The great tragedy of life doesn't lie in failing to reach your goals. The great tragedy lies in having no goals to reach." I was so blessed to be guided by a father who demanded I strive for higher heights and deeper depths. If I am satisfied with what I have, I have already achieved all I want out of life. For me, that would mean that there is no real incentive to work for more.

Impediments face each of us. Nobody ever promised an easy road or one not filled with bumps. All Christians recognize the trials and tribulations that Jesus faced while here on earth. As His followers we can expect the same. The test comes with remaining steadfast throughout the difficulties until we realize victory. Find promise in the words of Oliver Wendell Holmes. "What lies behind us and what lies before us are tiny matters compared to what lies within us" (Howe 2003, 240).

If *My Father's Faith* encourages at least one person, I have fulfilled my purpose. If the message uplifts at least one, I have completed my mission. If one finds more tenacity to fight the good fight, my struggle has been worth it. If one decides to seek higher aspirations, it has been worth my efforts to put this into print. Finally, if one increases his or her faith in God, the kingdom rejoices.

Matthew 17 reminds us of Jesus's words to His disciples after they failed to bring healing to a man's son that the scripture describes as a lunatic, one vexed with a spirit. The father brought the boy to Jesus because the disciples could not help him. Jesus rebuked the devil, and it exited the child immediately. The disciples, naturally perplexed, asked why they were unable to cast out the spirit.

Jesus's reply was profound. He explained the cause of their failure. "Because of your unbelief: for verily I say unto you, if you have faith as a grain of mustard seed, ye shall say unto this mountain, Remove hence to yonder place; and it shall remove; and nothing shall be impossible unto you. Howbeit this kind goeth out by prayer and fasting" (Matt. 17:20–21).

At an early age, I concluded that I needed a dose of what I refer to as "mustard seed faith." Allow me to explain my rationale. When I feel weak or sick in the natural, I go to my doctor. She writes a prescription for medicine to attack the symptoms I have described. That is, I seek the wisdom of one who has the expertise to deal with my physical ailments.

My mustard seed faith allows me to go to God through faith to make provisions for me in spite of my failings. I have an advocate constantly pleading my case in the person of Jesus Christ, the Great Physician. He knows all about my sicknesses, diseases, sources of anxiety, causes of distress, and shortcomings because He made me. "God hath dealt to every man the measure of faith" (Rom. 11:3). It is up to me to use the faith I have and grow it, just like a mustard seed.

Mustard seeds begin as very tiny grains. They must be placed in the ground, watered, and allowed to grow. The seeds absorb the water they have been planted in and produce leaves in two to three days. By that time they are ready to handle whatever weather conditions they might face. Mustard seed faith matures in much the same way. This faith begins small because it is just a measure of faith. It will continue to flourish as we pray, trust God, and get closer to Him. Our faith permits us to handle the storms and tempests that we face as Christians. It keeps us grounded when the raging winds blow in the spiritual, and natural, realm. If you have never found yourself in the midst of the storms of life, keep living. They will come.

The father in this scripture went to Jesus in order to alleviate the boy's suffering. His son's condition remained unchanged even after the disciples prayed. Jesus reminded the disciples of His teaching. He said, "If they had faith the size of a mustard seed, they could say to the mountain to be thou removed and the same would occur" (Matt. 17:20). Jesus told them that they were unable to cast out the spirit because of their unbelief. He took this opportunity to teach a valuable lesson. The disciples needed to do more than just pray.

Jesus rebuked the deaf and dumb spirit and commanded it to come out of the boy and enter him no more. Even when Jesus spoke to the spirit, it cried out and convulsed the boy greatly, but it came out of him. The boy went rigid, as if he were dead, but Jesus took him by the hand and lifted him up. And the child arose. When we encounter great mountains in life before us, it is time to fast and pray.

Do you have to fast and pray? In my opinion, if you want to be successful in God, prayer and fasting are essential to growth. They are the rudiments of spiritual discipline and pertinent channels in the faith-building process. My father taught that there were benefits to fasting and praying. He would call for fasts in our church and explain the procedure to be followed. Sometimes a fast would be for a few hours; other times for a day or two. Dad said we should always fast and pray with an intentional prayer in mind. That is what I learned, and that is what I do.

This boy's deliverance was the direct result of this principle. Prayer freed Peter from prison. The prayer of faith heals the sick and forgives sin. James 5:16 tells us, "The effective fervent prayer of a righteous man avails much." We are required to pray. A strong prayer life reinforces religious foundations. Everything rises or falls on your ability to touch heaven.

Christians should begin each day with prayers asking God to prepare us to remain unfaltering as we enter the spiritual battle. That is why it is necessary to put on the whole armor of God to become empowered to stand. The campaigns we wrestle with are not against "flesh and blood, but against principalities, against powers, against the rulers of the darkness of this world, against spiritual wickedness in high places" (Eph. 6:12). The apostle Paul cautions, "Praying always with all prayer and supplication in the Spirit" (Eph. 6:18). Christians come to understand writer A.W. Tozer's belief that the world is a battleground, not a playground.

When Jesus spoke about fasting, He didn't say, "If you fast." He said, "When you fast." Andrew Murray expressed, "Fasting helps to express, to deepen, and to confirm the resolution that we are ready to sacrifice anything—to sacrifice ourselves—to attain what we seek for the kingdom of God" (www.beliefnet.com/Quotes/Christian/A/Andrew-Murray.aspx).

By fasting, we demonstrate that we are seeking God with all our hearts. In my opinion we fast to mortify or kill our flesh, to bring us closer to God's will as we listen to His voice, and to commit our bodies to worship. It is true that you can pray without fasting, but you cannot fast without praying. When you fast without praying, you are just hungry.

Chapter 2:
A SYNOPSIS OF MY FATHER AND MY FAMILY

Faith expects from God what is beyond all expectation.
—Andrew Murray (Rhodes 2011, 85)

Who could have believed that an African American from the poorer side of a western Pennsylvania city would one day become principal of the nation's oldest existing junior high school? That same woman of color would later serve as the first African American principal of the city's senior high school in its 150-year history. When the junior and senior high schools were combined on one campus, this blessed woman of God was selected as its leader.

My father, the late Reverend Israel L. Gaither, believed that aspirations could be achieved and there were no limits to success. He interpreted both literally and spiritually Paul's statement to the Philippians, "I can do all things through Christ which strengthens me" (Phil. 4:13).

Born in 1913, my father began his life in what he referred to as "the red hills of North Carolina." His grandparents, Elijah Gaither and Laura Clements Gaither, were former slaves. Their marriage was the foundation of the Gaither-Clements' legacy in Mocksville, North Carolina, just outside of the city of Winston-Salem. The Clements' slave owners established a school for the slaves' children. The black children from the Clements' plantation were the first generation of my kinfolk to come out of slavery with an education. Two intersecting streets named after the families recognize their influence in the community.

My father's parents, Israel Lee Gaither and Carmilla Nichols Gaither, had eight children. The family, like many other black families in the area, emphasized strong religious conviction, hard work, and education. My aunts attended college, but my dad and his brothers were expected to find employment outside of the home.

In his early years, Dad picked tobacco and cotton to earn money and later worked as a chauffeur for a wealthy family. In spite of his circumstances, he managed to attend two years at Livingstone College in Salisbury, North Carolina, before leaving the South.

Longing for a better life, Israel Gaither left North Carolina during the Great Depression. He settled in Pennsylvania in 1936. His older sister, Mary Gaither Meeks, encouraged his transition to the area. She was the wife of the pastor of the St. Luke African Methodist Episcopal (AME) Zion Church. She opened her home to him when he came to New Castle. Although there was an abundance of jobs in steel mills and plants, these positions did not pay substantial wages or benefits. He spent a large portion of his working years at the Radiator Works, later renamed the Crane Company.

He brought with him the fundamental teachings of his AME Zion upbringing. He married my mother, the former Lillian Johnson, on April 17, 1939, on the back porch of her father's home on Croton Avenue. The Johnsons were one of the few African American families living in that part of town. To this union were born five children: Israel Lee III, Carmilla, Judy, Jacqueline, and Kathy.

I am a product of humble beginnings. We lived in a five-room house with two bedrooms and one bathroom, but it was always spick-and-span clean. The mantel in the living room displayed high school graduation pictures. All of us wanted to graduate so we could claim a spot on the shelf. Everyone in the family was required to graduate. I'm not sure why there was a mantel; we didn't have a fireplace. It was still a nice addition to the room. Not accomplishing this level of achievement was never given a second thought. Graduation was regarded as the first step in the fostering of a successful future.

Dad did not want his son to work in a dirty mill. Each child was expected to climb high on the ladder of accomplishment. No height was impossible to reach. Once we left home and completed college, it was highly unlikely that any of us would come back to live permanently with our parents except under catastrophic conditions. Each was given the means to stand on his or her own.

My three sisters and I shared one bedroom. I often wonder why I hear people say on shows like *House Hunters* on HGTV that they want to buy the same type of house they grew up in. Our house was extremely small. It was a tiny dwelling before they became popular on television. In those days I could never have imagined living in a home with a master bedroom and an attached bathroom, an air-conditioned house, or one with temperature control at the touch of a finger.

A coal furnace was the source of our warmth. We waited patiently for my father to stoke the ashes and add some lumps of coal to give us heat in the morning. The big coal truck would come regularly and fill an area of the basement with new fuel. That furnace also produced a great deal of dust, which I discovered as the cause of my constant sneezing. It also provided the reason for daily dusting in the house. We would stand over the floor registers to get extra heat. Nothing could compare to those hot blasts after coming in from the cold. My mother could often be spotted standing over the register eating ice cream.

In the large backyard, my father planted a garden. A grape arbor and weeping willow trees graced the land. My father worked the garden to ensure fresh vegetables were on the table. What wasn't eaten then was canned for a later date. Grapes were made into jelly. I don't know of anyone in my neighborhood who went hungry in those days.

My sisters and I each had two drawers in the dresser and one-fourth of the hanging closet for our clothes. That wasn't a problem though because we didn't have many clothes to put in them. Receiving a bike was a big deal. We looked forward to stockings filled with apples, oranges, and walnuts on Christmas morning. Gifts for birthdays and Christmases usually contained something to wear, along with a few toys as a plus.

My older sisters passed down their good clothes to me as they got more. I was happy to receive them. In my mind, wearing their clothes made me as sophisticated as they were.

My brother spent his nights on a pullout sofa bed. He was nine years old when I was born and thirteen when Kathy came. She was so little when he left for Salvation Army Training School in New York City. When he came home, Kathy wanted to know who this visitor was. Because of the great distance between New York and Pennsylvania, he only traveled on major holidays. When he did come, we all knew that the son had returned. Everyone was excited. Mother baked pies and cooked his favorite meals.

Dinners were always family time. Suppers did not always contain meat, but we certainly got full when we sat down. Beans or greens (cooked in ham hocks) and cornbread, topped off with buttermilk, were very satisfying meals. Dad was from the South, so oxtails, pig feet, and neck bones were a frequent choice. On special holidays Mother would clean and cook chitterlings (hog intestines). She said grocers used to give them away until they realized that black folks would buy them. My sister Kathy still prepares these dishes.

When Dad went fishing, the main course was seafood. If he went hunting, rabbit or pheasant could show up on the menu. Once Dad killed a "possem" while hunting and brought it home. Mother cooked it and then gave him a sandwich in his lunch the next day. He had a fit, but another man gave him fifty cents for the wild game. He never killed another one that I knew of.

My father didn't hunt big game; venison was not part of our meals unless another hunter donated it. My parents would try to convince us that it was roast beef, but we knew better. Once a man dropped off a live piglet in a burlap sack. Dad killed it, dressed it, and cooked it, but we refused to eat it. That was just a little too fresh. To this day I only eat meat with "USDA" stamped on it. Dad said every part of the pig was used or eaten on the farm. The only thing that got away was the squeal.

The girls received baby chicks one Easter as a gift. They kept growing and getting fat. One day we noticed the chickens were gone and fried chicken was the meal that night. We took the chicken off the serving tray and buried the meat in the backyard. Dad never admitted that our dinner was our pets.

On Sundays roast beef or fried chicken was cooked. It wasn't considered a Sunday meal if one of the two were not served. If preachers were visiting the church or people came from out of town, they were usually invited to partake in the meal. One lady and her family devoured our food like it was their Last Supper. Then she said she needed meat in order to eat her dessert.

Mother always made sure her kids had pieces of the white meat. There were no legs or thighs for us unless that was our choice. One would be surprised how many people requested the neck of the chicken or even the feet. Everyone ate together and shared the happenings of the day. We were never excused from the table until all the food on the plate was eaten.

My mother did not prepare two or three different dishes to accommodate our tastes. We ate what was served and better not have any complaints about what we didn't like. My sister Carmilla hated green peas. She would hold them in her mouth and pretend to eat them. She sat at the table for extended periods of time. The peas would find their way into a napkin much later. I vowed I would only eat what I liked when I got older. That is one promise I have kept, even though, unlike my sister, peas are one of my favorite vegetables.

As children, we were never allowed to open the refrigerator or cupboards at will and take what we wanted. We had to make a formal request, and we did not take any action until a reply was given. If we asked for a cookie, the answer was usually to take two. If we asked for a bowl of cereal, that was exactly what we got. My parents would never allow us to eat two or three bowls of cereal at a time. Many mornings Mother prepared cream of wheat or oatmeal. Hot cereal was very filling and stayed with us until lunchtime.

Meals were carefully planned; snacks had to last until the next shopping trip. My parents bought groceries every two weeks because that was how Dad was paid. Lunches also had to be prepared for school. We were not denied food. We were simply taught to be polite and respect the fact that an entire family had to eat from that which was available.

There was only one phone, the home phone. We had the same phone number as long as I could remember. It went from Oliver 2-6423 to 652-6423 and, finally, (724) 652-6423. The number remained with the Gaither family until my mother's final days. No one ever wasted time on the phone.

We didn't have a garage for the car, just a space between the houses where we parked our auto. We were happy to have a vehicle. From what I can remember, there wasn't a garage on our street.

Neighbors were family. If we wanted to eat dinner at their homes, a place was created. One of our neighbor's sons always referred to my mother as "Mother." He loved her spaghetti and was sure to be there at dinnertime when it was served.

We sat out on the porch until late in the evening, enjoying the cool breezes in the summer. Occasionally we could hear the sounds of young men harmonizing on the corner or playing basketball on the court up the street. People took walks after dusk, never fearing for their lives.

Adults were never called by their first name. A "handle" had to be affixed as their title. Miss, Missus, Mister, Aunt, or Uncle would be the likely choices. Many people addressed as Aunt or Uncle were not a member of the bloodline. It was simply a method of giving respect.

I am flabbergasted when I have to correct young people who attempt to call me by my given name. For example, I was in a bank one day, and a former student referred to me in that manner.

When I confronted him, he said, "I'm grown now."

I said, "Then just consider me as a customer who desires to be spoken to with respect."

I still do not call my former teachers by any name other than Mister or Missus, even though I became their supervisor. I was taught that in polite society the only way a person was called by his or her first name was if that person asked you to do so.

The girls had to be at home when the streetlights came on; it was different for my brother. Once my mother called one of us, she listed all of us by name, starting from the oldest to the youngest. If we were distracted while playing, we would come running whenever we heard her voice. It was a time that we always felt safe and secure. We really didn't need to lock the doors during the day. No one ever thought of breaking into houses or cars. The front door was always open during the day to allow cool breezes through the screen door. We lifted windows in the summer because we didn't have air-conditioning. Passersby greeted us as if they had known us all our lives.

Everyone knew where the preacher lived. Sometimes a stranger would pull up to our house and ask if the minister living there could perform a marriage ceremony. My father would never marry two people without counseling them first. There was a reverence for the ministry during those days. No one would swear or use profanity near our house. If young men wanted to throw dice or play cards, they did it away from the neighbors because they knew the behavior would be reported back to their parents.

Since we attended a neighborhood school, we came home for lunch. Most mothers were stay-at-home moms, and a hot meal awaited their children. The close proximity to the elementary school also meant that a parent could show up at any moment, especially if a student had gotten into trouble during class.

I had two cousins who were the same age as me, and we were in the same classroom. If my mother or her sisters (Aunt Willie Barker or Aunt Theodosia Terry) came to the school for any reason, we all were put "in check." They were entitled to correct any of the children as needed without any question.

All our families were close. Many of my cousins are like siblings to me. Precious bonds were formed during those years that still exist today.

My father spent quality time with his children, teaching and nurturing them. He was the epitome of what a father should be and do. He lived his testimony, and his example has been passed down to his progeny. Every summer we made the twelve-hour trip to North Carolina to visit his father. There were no super highways, only hills, mountains, and two-lane roads. We always drove straight through. There was no money for motels and probably few that would accept an African American family, if we did.

Mother got up early ("before day in the morning," as she called it), fried the chicken, and packed a basket for the trip. Most of the chicken would be gone by the time we reached West Virginia about two hours away. Whenever we stopped for gas, Dad would always first ask if they permitted his family to use the restrooms at the station. If they refused, we went further until we found a more accommodating gas station.

Dad's eldest sister was one of the best cooks in my world. I loved that fried corn she made. Her house was the oldest, and her kitchen was the smallest, but her home was always the most inviting. She cooked those wonderful meals on a woodstove in the middle of her kitchen. As my parents got older, my husband and I took them to see the relatives there.

When Aunt Mary visited from Chicago, we felt like the queen of England had arrived. Her Estée Lauder perfume enveloped the atmosphere, and her distinctive laugh was contagious. A very distinguished-looking woman, she wore extravagant hats to church. I developed my love of chapeaus from her. Her life is still celebrated in the AME Zion denomination.

Our family enjoyed picnics at Cascade Park, Idora Amusement Park, and Conneaut Lake Park. Dad was never afraid of the roller coaster rides, no matter how steep they were. Once the coaster at a park stopped on the hill. My father walked up the wooden enclosure and carried my sister and me to safety. He didn't wait for the park to take action. He would often convince church members that the roller coasters were not scary. Then we would all howl when we saw folks screaming! One church lady even lost her wig on a ride. It flew off as the coaster came speeding down.

At church picnics he could be seen playing baseball and participating in the sack race. He ran faster than most men half his age. We fed the fish at the causeway at Pymatuning Lake while Dad would take the opportunity to throw in his line. In the fall the family would take long rides to see the changing of the leaves.

Reverend Gaither never got a salary for being a pastor. He often donated the difference if there were a shortage of money in the offering. Sometimes people would bring canned goods or meat as a means of showing their love. They called it giving him "pounds." I am not sure where that term originated, but the food did put extra weight on us.

We appreciated receiving large government tins of peanut butter from members the most. My sister Judy and I would make gigantic peanut butter cookies. We should have patented them before the cookie stores in the malls came up with the idea much later.

Praying and studying consumed my father's late nights. Someone once called him "the weeping prophet" because he shed so many tears while singing or preaching. He often began his invocation (prayer) using the words of Isaac Watts (1719):

> Oh Lord, our God, our help in ages past,
> Our hope for years to come,
> Our shelter from the stormy blast,
> And our eternal home.

In 1971 my parents moved to a larger home on the eastern side of the city. The move came the same year I began college. Only my sister Kathy continued to live with them. My older siblings had already left home for college or careers. A city rehabilitation project bought the homes on one side of West North Street, and a new configuration of roads was developed. Oddly enough the land on which our house had sat for years was now deemed unfit to rebuild on. The neighborhood family was now dispersed to all parts of town.

We were never aware that we were considered poor in an economic sense. My mother only worked outside of the home sporadically. She was employed at the Shenango Pottery early in her life. She also cleaned houses on the other side of town. She later became a cook for a county-wide food program. The only problem was that she tried foods on us that she cooked for Meals on Wheels. We expected a sweet potato pie for holidays. She made a raisin pie instead one Christmas. I can still hear her brother say to her, "Sister, what in the world is this?"

To put it simply, if we were poor, we didn't know it. Everyone in our neighborhood had as much or as little as we did. As children we didn't know that anyone else lived any differently. We were never hungry or homeless. We always had clean clothes and forever trusted the Lord. We focused on the love we shared as a family and the time we spent together. The family's economic standing was not the children's concern. We were content with the love we shared as a unit.

Rooted and grounded in his faith, Dad raised his family through hard work, true grit, and fortitude. Most days he would leave his job at the mill and earn extra money mowing lawns or simonizing (waxing) cars. He believed in working hard and saving money. Unfortunately saving money was not a trait I acquired from him. He accumulated money and often hid it in the house.

He once bought a car and put so much down on it that the payment was only thirty dollars a month. He told me that he made three or four payments each month after that to quickly pay off the vehicle. He insisted I do the same thing. I laughed. I could barely make the one payment that I sent to the bank each month.

After living through the Great Depression, he didn't trust banks fully and never had a lot of credit cards. Nor did he think that he should co-sign for anyone for anything. His maxim was, "Work hard, save your money, and buy whatever you want outright with cash."

Dad would, however, give the kids anything he had if there were a need. When he visited our colleges or before we returned to school, he always placed a love offering in our hands. Even when we were adults, he would often slip us a few dollars. Like King David, he could say with assurance, "I once was young and now am old; yet have I not seen the righteous forsaken, nor his seed begging bread" (Ps. 37:25).

When he was not working at the Crane Company, he was working for the Lord. Hard work was an attribute that was emphasized in our family. If you wanted something out of life, you had to work for it. Laziness was not tolerated. We were raised doing chores in the home and then finding jobs when we came of age.

My sister Judy worked in a clothing store called Betty Gay's. She never brought much of her paycheck home because she was always putting clothes on layaway. I ironed in the home of an elderly Jewish couple before working at a grocery store. Those jobs convinced me that I needed to obtain a higher education. After a customer slammed a can of vegetables down on a coworker's hand because it wasn't on sale, I was certain that I could not stay in that job forever. I felt good bringing home a few groceries or giving a small monetary contribution to the household. There was definitely no sitting around in the Gaither household.

Before we got a real job, we spent most summers working at the local Salvation Army camp, Camp Allegheny, just ten or so miles from where we lived. There, my brother developed a relationship with the Salvation Army. We all started as campers before becoming employees.

Depending on our age, we could work in the cafeteria, be a camp counselor, or take whatever job was available within our qualifications. We spent evenings around the campfire singing religious songs, some of which I still sing to my grandchildren. At the end of the summer, I could buy my own clothes for the upcoming school year, as long as they were not jeans. Blue jeans reminded my father of the clothes he wore while picking tobacco in the fields. He never permitted his children to wear them for that reason.

I continued to work at the grocery store during college holidays when I came home and even after I started teaching. When I cashed my first teacher's paycheck there, the head teller laughed aloud. She grossed more than I did with a four-year education. The job met my needs for a season. Thank God that season passed.

If we told my dad that we were bored, he brought out the push lawn mower to relieve the condition. From what I can remember, there were no riding or power mowers back then. We couldn't afford one in the event they did exist. If we told him we wanted to go for a walk, the lawn mower came out again, and he would say to walk behind it while cutting the grass.

We recognized a strong work ethic at an early age. My father taught us that there were no entitlements in this life in the natural. We are, however, beneficiaries of the blessings of God, our Father in the spiritual. One of his favorite scriptures was from Genesis 3:19 when God told Adam, "By the sweat of your brow, you shall eat." In other words, if a man didn't work, he didn't eat. Since we all loved to eat my mother's fried chicken, collard greens, and especially her sweet potato pie, it was incumbent on each of us to share in the workload.

That meant the girls were assigned daily chores around the house. My brother was expected to assist Dad with the outside chores. The completion of the tasks was not debatable. In the spring, we washed walls with some kind of putty and completely overhauled the dwelling. All curtains were taken down, washed, and ironed. Mattresses were reversed on the beds; major cleaning was undertaken in every room of the house.

We didn't have an automatic washer back then. The wringer washer sat in the basement for our use. We did not get paid to do household tasks. That was a responsibility we each had. Each child received a small weekly allowance, part of which we gave to the church as tithes. Yes, we were taught that 10 percent of what we received went back to God. That is why I am blessed today. The Bible teaches that we are blessed by our giving.

God says in Malachi 3:10, "Bring ye all the tithes into the storehouse, that there may be meat in mine house, and prove me now herewith, saith the Lord of hosts, if I will not open you the windows of heaven, and pour you out a blessing, that there shall not be room enough to receive it."

I wanted those kinds of blessings, the ones I could not contain. I yearned for those that I didn't have enough room to receive. And notice that the scripture reads "windows," as in plural. That means that abundance flows freely from many sources. The concept of giving allowed me to find prosperity in my life. The blessings I sought, however, were not simply monetary. Genesis 12:1–3 records God's promises to Abraham.

> Go forth from your country, and from your relatives and from your father's house, to the land which I will show you; and I will make you a great nation, and I will bless you, and make your name great; and so you shall be a blessing; and I will bless those who bless you, and curse those who curse you. And in you all the families of the earth shall be blessed.

Abraham's acquisition of these possibilities was based on his faithfulness to follow the plan that God had set before him. They were conditional. Our blessings are not a result of luck; nor are they the notions of a psychic or medium. As the seed of Abraham, we are all entitled to the fulfillment of God's plan, which is ultimately designed to bring glory to Him. Once we acknowledge that what we have comes from the Lord and not of our own doing, we can graciously return it to Him and His ministries.

We were members of the Union Baptist Church. Dad served as a Sunday school teacher and deacon. He was called into the field of evangelism and was eventually ordained as a Baptist preacher. In 1962 he founded a church and became its pastor. The ministry began as a study in the homes of a few residents in the area and was called the "True Light Prayer and Bible Band." The preaching was charismatic, and the prayers were mighty. Songs were sung a cappella; there were no organs or drums back then. A few of the women would play the tambourine to the beat of the music. Foot stomping and hand clapping maintained the rhythm. The voices blended together harmoniously, reminding me of our African tradition.

The Holy Spirit was so high that it felt like the houses were shaking. We are a very vocal people and love to praise the Lord through song and spiritual dance, which we call shouting. If attendees agreed with the Word, they just hollered out "Amen," "say that," or "preach, preacher, preach" at will. (It is frequently referred to as call-and-response worship.)

Folks traveled to the prayer meetings from nearby communities. Others walked to be included in the worship service. The sounds of praise drew in people from the streets. The anointing was so awesome that lives were changed in a matter of minutes. The ministry was nondenominational, and the teachings were rooted in God's Word, which is always right.

As the numbers of worshippers increased, a church building was needed. A small structure located at 703 Sampson Street was rented for many years. The first formal service for the House of Prayer, often referred to as "the little house by the side of the road," was on October 14, 1962. Founder's Day is an annual celebration on the second Sunday of October. The name of the church came from Mark 11:17 when Jesus said, "And my house shall be called a house of prayer for all nations."

For nearly twenty years, the church broadcast live over WKST radio station every Sunday night. Dad would hold a portable radio to his ear and listen for the commentator to announce the service. The whole church would sit quietly until he gave the signal to begin singing, "The Lord Is Blessing Me Right Now." Nobody would ever break the silence until told to do so. Testimonies, singing, praying, and preaching filled the half hour. The radio broadcast proved to be an inspiration, not only to members, but also to those listening who were confined to their homes because of illness. It was a permanent fixture for two decades.

The church would sometimes receive small donations in the mail from people who had been uplifted by the broadcast.

Reverend Gaither was also well known in the city because of his melodious voice. He was the founder and lead singer of the Keystone Quartet, who recorded several albums in the 1940s. He continued to sing in church services as I grew up. The Quartet songs remain in my memory because my father sang them with new background singers. Mr. Roy Hambrick Sr. had a tremendous tenor voice. He joined the church and continued to sing. He was an original member of the Quartet and became one of the first deacons. Deacon Hambrick's son, Elder Gaird Hambrick, an accomplished guitarist, accepted the Lord as his Savior and donated his musical talent to the ministry for nearly fifty years. I was honored to be one of his backup singers when I became an adult.

As only he could, Dad would sing, "I'm on my way to Canaan Land. I'm on my way. Praise God. I'm on my way." His voice could bring me to tears because he was genuinely sincere about the message of Christianity.

He believed in the power of prayer and the ability of men and women to live holy lives through God's Word. Attending services at the Kathryn Kuhlman Ministry in Pittsburgh, Pennsylvania, was always a treat. Kuhlman was known for healing crusades across the nation. During each service Kuhlman would say, "I believe in miracles because I believe in God."

My father's faith caused him to believe in God's omnipotence to perform miracles. I know of people who came to our church just so my father could pray for them. I was told that my mother was in the hospital and the nurse could not hear her pulse. My father put forth a prayer of faith. Once the doctor came in, my mother was alert. The doctor scolded the nurse for an unnecessary call.

Another time a woman called our house and asked my father to come and pray for her. He went to her home and called on heaven. She got stronger and soon began attending church services. I observed many miracles with my own eyes and recognized God's healing virtues.

We had a strict upbringing in some people's opinion. We went to church whenever a service was scheduled. There was no just saying we were sick. Mother simply gave us a dose of castor oil, and then Dad anointed our foreheads with oil and prayed. We didn't play cards or bingo (which was considered gambling), dance (hence the reason I have no rhythm to this day), and watch movies (except for the viewing of the Three Stooges during my father's mill Christmas party). And the list goes on.

If we asked to go to a high school prom, my father said he would look in the window to be sure we weren't dancing. If we wanted to go to a high school football game on Friday, we definitely had to go to Bible study on Tuesday night. He always picked us up before the game ended to avoid the traffic, he maintained. I just figured he didn't want us to socialize too much. Ironically, as principal of a high school, my job included supervision of both football games and school dances.

One of my uncles took me to a drive-in theatre when I was about ten years old. As we pulled in, I began to shed tears.

He asked, "Why are you crying?"

I naïvely replied, "You get pregnant in the drive-in."

I thought all you had to do was pull in through the arches and become instantly pregnant! Yes, I was naïve, but that proved for my good as well.

Those elementary teachings stayed with me. It did not hurt me that I did not attend all dances. I still do not and cannot play cards to this day. My father was very protective and loving. He tried to shelter us from the dangers of this life. He was afraid for his children because of what he had witnessed growing up. I am grateful for that.

Reverend Gaither, an avid outdoorsman, loved to hunt and fish, activities he learned in his youth so he could put food on the table. Once when he was fishing on Lake Erie, my mother fell off a stepladder and broke her back. The local police contacted the authorities there to find him and make him aware of the situation. The police escorted him into our town. My mother recovered fully, but it seemed she was always falling. When she hurt herself, I somehow became the designated family cook. In the future those cooking lessons proved to be very useful.

Because of his love for hunting, guns were always in our home. He proudly displayed the rifles on a wall rack in the dining room. He often cleaned them whenever the girls had any male visitors, just a subtle message to would-be suitors that my father did not play. I really thought that I might become an old maid because of those guns.

The family planned a grand celebration for my parents' golden wedding anniversary. They renewed their vows with my brother officiating. I sent a letter beforehand to the White House, requesting a special message from the President of the United States, George H. W. Bush. I was unaware that special requests were supposed to go through the Greetings Office.

Time was drawing near, and I had not heard from the White House. I called and left a message, giving my parents' name and the event date. A few days later while I was teaching, I was summoned to the office for a phone call. (In those days we did not have phones in the classrooms.)

I answered the phone. The voice informed me that I would receive the greeting overnight and I was not to worry. I never included my place of work or the school's phone number in my previous correspondence with them.

When I asked how I was located, she replied, "Ma'am, this is the White House."

No more needed to be said. The message came as promised.

One of the surprises I had planned was to have them arrive in a limousine. It was April, and most of the companies were fully booked because of prom season. I wanted them to have this experience since the only way black people usually rode in a limo was when they were the family of a deceased person.

While eating lunch in the dining room at my school, one of my father's good friends came in and sat down. He asked me how the plans were going, and I proceeded to tell him my dilemma.

Looking at me in a serious manner, he asked, "Why didn't you just ask me? I'd do anything for my friend."

My father's dear friend, Mr. Edward DeCarbo, owned one of the largest funeral homes in the city and had a fleet of cars. He assured me that a car would come and take my parents to the vow renewal, which he would be attending as well. God worked out things again.

My parents renewed their vows, and the ceremony concluded with my brother saying, "And now you may kiss my mother."

Reverend Gaither remained in active ministry until his health declined and he was no longer able to attend services. Mother slept downstairs on the couch for seven years to be near his hospital bed located in the family room. She attended to his every need. I would bring our son Jonathan over when he was little, and he would sit on the bed with my dad. They both enjoyed reading the newspaper and watching their favorite television show, *Little House on the Prairie*. They would crack up laughing when the little girl, Laura Ingalls, fell down the hill in the opening segment, every time it came on!

My husband, the Reverend Torrance Respress, succeeded my father as pastor of the House of Prayer. Our immediate family was at Dad's bedside when he took his last breath on January 31, 1996. It was ironic that we were all there because my brother and sister lived in distant cities. Daddy had often related the story of his mother's passing from tuberculosis. He told us many times about how she called all her children to her bedside to give final directives for their future lives. They were advised to have faith and trust in God, the same message that my father passed on to us throughout his lifetime.

My father's intense dedication to and application of God's principles made him a model for Christians, both old and young. He was an insightful teacher and exceptional pastor. He was deeply hurt when many of the founding members came up with the idea that they needed a bigger church and a better preacher and walked away from the church. These men and women had urged him to begin the ministry and vowed to be congregants forever. One woman referred to our church as kindergarten and said she needed to move up to a high school experience. Throughout my life I have found few preachers that could expound on the Word like my own father.

The original congregation was comprised of a number of people who had never attended church or had a personal experience with Christ before the House of Prayer Ministry. Others came because of their desire to grow spiritually. They recognized the power and anointing of God in this place of worship. My father did not believe in stealing sheep (members) from other churches. Rather he felt his destiny was to reach out to the unsaved in the hedges and highways, as the scriptures dictated. Dad frequently donated money to help with rent, utilities, clothes, and food when others asked him for help. And he was always willing to assist those in need. What little he had he shared with the members and community. He was wounded but not defeated.

The words of Paul's Second Epistle to the Corinthians seem to aptly apply to him. "We are troubled on every side, yet not distressed; we are perplexed, but not in despair; persecuted, but not forsaken; cast down but not destroyed" (2 Cor. 4:8–9).

My father continued to press on for the kingdom's sake. The church did not fold, as some had predicted and perhaps even desired. There were those who had expected the doors to close within six months of being established. God proved them wrong. It continues to thrive in its original location, "by the side of the road." We endured. A number of ministers were licensed and ordained through the House of Prayer. Dad was regarded as a father and mentor by those he came in contact with.

My father instilled basic ideas of tithing, prayer, fasting, worship, and praise to his children. Those teachings motivated me in my career path. I too trusted the words of Joshua 1:8. "For then they shalt make thy way prosperous, and thou shall have good success." That scripture provided a strategic resource in this fight called life. There's no need to go to battle on your own.

Second Chronicles 20:15 notes, "Be not afraid nor dismayed by reason of this great multitude; for the battle is not yours, but God's." The bigger the opponent, the greater the reliance on my faith.

Because of my father, the words of the scripture texts came alive on the pages as I memorized them. My mother and father read and studied the Bible diligently each day. No meal was begun without a family prayer and the recitation of a passage from each of us. Verses were picked from small cards that were included in the symbolic Loaf of Bread, a small container shaped like a loaf of bread. It remained on the dinner table at all times. I credit those cards with my ability to recite scriptures today. We did not end the day without a prayer before bedtime.

Scriptures are regarded as one of my weapons of spiritual warfare when circumstances require heavenly intervention. Once memorized, the verses became my personal arsenal. No one could take them from me.

Dad's prolific recollection of scriptures was impressive; he developed a love of God's Word. Passages from the Bible would roll from his mouth like water. An injection of a verse at just the right time in his conversation was not unusual. For instance, if a member were eating at a church dinner and acting like it was his or her last meal (i.e., very greedily), my father would ask, "Have you not houses to eat in?" (1 Cor. 11:22). And everyone would burst into laughter.

Even as he got older, Dad had a tremendous memory. The proof was in the ability to recite Paul Laurence Dunbar's poems that he had learned in his segregated schoolhouse as a child. Dunbar, a celebrated African American poet, playwright, and novelist of the late nineteenth and early twentieth century, wrote in both conventional English and Negro dialect. The vernacular is reminiscent of how slaves would talk.

Dunbar's parents had been slaves. My father could recall many of the verses until he became ill. His favorites were "In the Morning" and "When Malindy Sings." Not only would he say the words in dialect, he would act them out.

"In the Morning" tells the story of a young man who does not want to get out of bed and the tongue lashing he gets from his mother for his inactivity. It begins: "Lias! Lias! Bless de Lawd! Don' you know de day's erbroad. Ef you don't git up, you scamp. Dey'll be trouble in this camp" (Dunbar, 1913, 190). Just pronouncing the words is difficult for most people.

The young, unsaved Israel Gaither was a great dancer. Mother said people would move back to give him room. He stood only five foot nine, but he was very distinguished looking and had a special presence about himself that commanded attention and respect. And in my opinion, he was one handsome man. His steel grey eyes could look right through people. He could eyeball a person and set him or her straight.

He also smoked cigarettes in his early years. Once he found out that my mother was pregnant with my brother, he threw away his cigarettes and never smoked again in his life. He trusted God for his deliverance from that form of bondage. There was no gum or patches to stop smoking back then. He simply turned his habit over to God. He believed that dancing and smoking hindered his Christian walk and his testimony. He could attest to God's power to bring him through.

The Gaither children were never asked if we would attend college. That was assumed. The only question asked was, "Which college will you attend?" If we didn't matriculate at the Salvation Army School for

Officer Training (of which my brother Israel Lee and sister Carmilla attended), geography limited our choices. We had to choose a college within thirty minutes of our home, so he, as he told us, could check on us. And we had better be studying when he got there. That kept me studying all the time! I had a genuine fear that I would disappoint him. The fear I mention was not the same as being afraid. It was respect.

After Dad's death, Mother tried to stay in the family home, but it soon became too much for her. Visits and phone calls were incorporated into my daily routine. Mother had never learned to drive, so we took her wherever she needed to go. We obviously needed to have her closer to us. She moved into our home and lived with us for sixteen years. My husband had previously remodeled the entire basement of our house with a private bedroom, bathroom, and living room. She said she wanted to be upstairs with us, so she chose a bedroom on the second floor. When ascending the stairs became a problem, we installed a chair lift to assist her movement.

Her using the bedroom close to me proved to be a godsend later on in her stay. Anytime she needed me and called for help, I could hear her and come to her bedside. She spent her last months in a nursing home because she was unable to walk and needed professional care. My mother entered the nursing home on June 19, 2012. That was the first time that my husband and I had ever lived alone together as a married couple. Akilah was with me when we married. Then Jonathan was born. Finally my mother lived with us.

I remember the date distinctly because it was our thirtieth wedding anniversary. We had planned to renew our wedding vows in Cancun with my son officiating but had to cancel because of her failing health.

I retired early from my position at the junior/senior high school so I could care for her as best I could. When she went to the nursing home, I visited her daily from nine o'clock in the morning until late in the evening when I put her to bed. My sister and brother visited frequently. Their visits allowed some respite time for me. The House of Prayer church family was also very supportive in her care. Members ensured she was never alone if I had to complete an errand or go to an appointment. My sister in the Lord, Judy Lockett, was always there when I needed her. Mother considered her as another daughter.

Following Mother's admittance to the nursing home, the nurse told me that her blood pressure was very low, as was her heart rate. He did not expect her to live more than a few days. She survived another three months and was comfortable until the end.

When Mother passed away, I made sure she looked like she was going to meet the King. We were always taught to dress in our finest clothes for church services. She explained, if we had been invited to the White House for dinner or Buckingham Palace for an audience with royalty, we would spare no expense to look our best for these earthly figures.

Now she was going to meet her Maker. She lived ninety-three years and was exhausted and weary. Orders were left not to resuscitate her if her heart failed. Mother was adamant that her wishes be carried out. She spent her last days sleeping until her breathing became labored. Eventually she just slipped away. My sister-in-law Eva and I were sitting in the room, and she said hesitantly, "I don't think Mother is breathing." She left this life peacefully.

My mother had fought a good fight and, like the Apostle Paul, was confident in her faith and preferred to be "absent from the body and at home with the Lord" (2 Cor. 4:8). Adorned with one of her favorite hats in the casket, she was attired in her Sunday best. One of the morticians told me he had never buried a woman with a fancy hat like the one she wore. No outfit would be complete without her jewelry, lap scarf, and purse. She always carried peppermints in her purse for church, so a few were inserted just in case. I made sure she had her nails done too, a French manicure.

A lovely home-going service was held in the church she had co-founded, the House of Prayer. Although she had never been ordained to preach, she played an integral role in the ministry. Her contributions were invaluable. The eulogist talked about her, Lillian Gaither, and her initials, "LG," and referred to the commercial slogan—"LG" or "Life is Good"—in his sermon. She had earned a crown of life.

She would often brag to her friends, "I don't do anything in my daughter's house. I am treated like a queen." She didn't need to do anything. She had spent her life caring for others. When she was young, she helped raise her siblings. She told me she could remember washing diapers when she was only five years old. She tended to her mother, who was very sick most of her life. I always wanted to ask why her mother kept having children if she were so sick, but I figured the question might be considered disrespectful. (I would still like an answer though.)

She often walked across town to look after her family once she got married. She practically raised all her younger brothers and sisters. She cooked for them, washed their clothes, and disciplined them when necessary. They treated her like she was their second mother. Her siblings lovingly nicknamed her "Sister," the term of endearment they used until her death on August 10, 2012.

These were the spiritual roots from which I came. The dictates of my father's Bible-based teachings guided my life. He was what they used to call a "hellfire and brimstone preacher." He presented an uncompromising gospel and refused to water it down, even if it meant that the numbers in our congregation remained small. Members of the House of Prayer were held accountable to the standard of living prescribed in God's Word. The strength of my spiritual life enabled me to be comforted through the loss of both of my parents and two sisters. Dad's unwavering faith sustained my belief.

Because of his insistence that we gain an education, all the children chose meaningful career paths. He would say, if we asked something of the Lord and had faith to believe it, the Lord would make it happen. My life is a testament of the life he lived. My brother, Salvation Army Commissioner Israel Gaither III, noted in his biography, *Man with a Mission* (Gariepy 2006, 10), that Dad would always remind him, "Remember your name. Remember who you are."

Ephesians 3:20 reminds us, "Now unto him that is able to do exceeding abundantly above all that we ask or think, according to the power that worketh in us." More faith means more power. Think higher!

Chapter 3:

MEMORIES FROM THE PAST

We are the inheritors of a past that gives us every reason to believe that we will succeed.
—A Nation At-Risk (1982)

I attended the same high school where I would later serve as principal. I must admit that pleasant memories did not always fill my high school years. In senior high school, we were tracked based on achievement levels. Tracking was from group one to group ten, and I was included in the highest track—group one. That meant I spent most of my classes with only a few students of color. It was definitely not cool to be smart back then. A few of the students assumed my schedule was a sign that I thought I was "uppity" or an "Aunt Jane," the reverse of an Uncle Tom.

Inwardly they might have been judgmental because I didn't attend parties, go skating, or do all the fun things they did. They did not realize that the Gaither children were not permitted to engage in those activities because of our household rules. Some of the white students were friendly, but I didn't visit their homes, and they didn't come to mine. It was simply what the times dictated.

I definitely lacked personal confidence in anything except my intellectual abilities. My skin was always very oily. Acne was my constant foe. I jokingly kidded a former star athlete that he never spoke to me in school. He denied my allegation, but I know the truth.

One day I was walking with a group of students in front of a room. One boy said my face shined like a lightbulb. Oddly enough, when I ran into him at an event many years later, the first thing I remembered were his hurtful comments to me. He, now a grown man, probably never gave his statement a second thought. That scene replayed itself numerous times in my head.

One never knows the damage that can be done to a person's self-esteem with the weapon called the tongue. When one is not part of the in crowd as a student, what one goes through can make a person either bitter or better. I chose better.

My self-image began to be restored as I watched how professional people acted and read stories on improvement. *Ebony* and *Jet* were always a fixture in our home. In college, a professor, a white woman, introduced me to *Vogue*. I studied the trends and developed a routine designed to improve my appearance. The high point of fashion was when I attended the Ebony Fashion Show that toured the country each year. Fortunately one of the annual stops was in Youngstown, Ohio. That oily skin eventually proved its worth. I have very few lines and wrinkles because of it.

During my early years, a statement was made in my presence that "black people were dirty and did not use soap." I knew firsthand that the description was untrue because of my own upbringing. Furthermore I worked in a grocery store and witnessed black people buying plenty of soap and detergent. Because I was outspoken even as a child, I challenged those views. Ironically I enrolled in a course later in life, and that same person was in the class. Taking the seat next to the man, now much older, and reminding him of my name, I told him I was not sixteen years old anymore with a smile. That man would not dare make such a statement to me now.

A friend from a nearby school district shared a story with me. Shortly before an annual program, he was informed he could not walk across the stage to receive his academic awards. He presumed the decision was made because of his race since he met high academic standards on every level and had earned the recognition. That situation did not serve as a deterrent. Instead he used the negative experience to propel him into a positive future.

An adult once tried to discourage my sister Judy from taking the Scholastic Aptitude Test (SAT), noting she was not college material. The SAT is one factor in determining a student's acceptance into college. She did in fact take the test and scored highly on it. Her test score was so impressive that she was offered a full scholarship to a Massachusetts university.

Judy related this story on many occasions and to various audiences to expose the judgments and pronouncements that others often place on aspiring black females. She was a person in which some saw no potential for college, yet she earned a bachelor's degree, two masters of education degrees in guidance and administration, and a doctor of philosophy degree in educational administration. In later life she was employed as an assistant superintendent and college professor at various colleges in Indiana and Ohio before her untimely passing.

My sister encouraged, cajoled, and sometimes even forced me to become a school administrator. Her death came one month before my graduation from the Youngstown State University with a master's degree and principal's certificate. I included this story to encourage those whose abilities may not be seen or encouraged by others. God has the plan and knows your potential!

Luke 8:43–47 relates the account of another woman who was persistent despite her obvious encumbrances.

> And a woman having an issue of blood 12 years, which had spent all her living upon the physicians, neither could be healed of any, came behind him, and touched the border of his garment; and immediately her issue of blood stanched. And Jesus said, Who touched me? When all denied, Peter and they that were with him said, Master, the multitude throng thee and press thee, and sayest thou, Who touched me? And Jesus said somebody hath touched me: for I perceive that virtue is gone out of me. And when the woman saw that she was not hid, she came

trembling, and falling down before him, she declared unto him before all the people for what cause she had touched him, and how she was healed immediately.

The writer of this text, a gifted physician, was more knowledgeable about cures for certain afflictions than most people in his day. Luke concluded that the unnamed woman could not be healed. In other words, he based his fatalistic diagnosis on his level of expertise and what he had previously studied. According to what he knew about medicine, she was a "walking" dead woman. What a pronouncement on a person's life!

How many times have we allowed others' voices to affect choices we make? They will tell you or indicate by their actions that they don't believe in you or you will never amount to anything. By man's benchmarks a death sentence was impending. By God's standards healing was forthcoming.

The extent of her infirmity describes the woman. She is first identified by her ailment, as one with "an issue of blood." Luke then defined her by the length of time she was ill, twelve years. Later she is referred to by her economic standing as a result of her disease. She was poor because she had given all she had in seeking a cure. It was a disease of the bloodstream affecting her female reproductive system. Her condition was so dreadful that she was rebuked by the community, declared unclean under ceremonial law, and segregated from society. Total healing would only be obtained if she could get close enough to Jesus to touch the source of her healing.

Another lesson can be learned from the text. The scripture outlines the process of her deliverance. She actively pursued it. The following is what I gathered from the verses: A desperate woman sought a solution to a tenuous situation and wouldn't take no for an answer. She is an example of persistence and faith in action. (Her perseverance could be compared, on some level, to the African American female experience in America.)

Faith that is not put into action is no faith at all. The Gaither children found we had to look beyond what others thought of us and press toward our intended goals. Like Apostle Paul, it was instilled in us to stretch out and chase our aspirations with all our might. There is virtue in the press.

Chapter 4:

A FEW OF THE MIRACLES IN MY LIFE

You are the God that performs miracles; you display your power among the peoples.
—Psalm 77:14 NIV

It goes without saying that miraculous things have happened in my life. Certainly the gift of life and breath, a "right" mind, and a reasonable portion of health and strength (as the older Pentecostal believers used to say) are among God's miracles each day. The fact I was able to teach and later be appointed as a principal in New Castle was unquestionably because of God. To this day the events of my life still amaze me. I could not possibly let this portion of my story end without sharing my personal experiences with my heavenly Father and His phenomenal, mind-blowing, marvelous capability to meet my needs. My faith in God allows me to ask for what I need and trust Him to receive. I am only touching the surface just to give a peek about what God can do. The reality is, what He does for others, He will do for you. Truthfully it truly is no secret what God can do.

When I was twenty years old, I needed to pass my driver's test so I could transport myself to complete the student teaching requisite of my degree. I did not need a driver's license before that time because I didn't have a car, my father didn't allow anyone except my brother to drive his car, and we weren't allowed to go anywhere.

One of my friends at Slippery Rock taught me to operate a car and took me to take the test on two separate occasions. After failing it both times, my father accompanied me the third time. When I was leaving the Department of Transportation area to begin my driving test, I noticed him bowing on his knees to pray. I passed. That was a miracle. I still don't know how to parallel park. Who does that anyway?

At the age of thirty, I became pregnant with our son Jonathan. At that time thirty was considered old to have a first child. When the obstetrician told me the results of my pregnancy test, I said I had the flu. He said we would see if I still had the flu in nine months. I had always been told that I was unable to have children. The pregnancy went well at first, and then I became seriously ill. Many nurses worked at the facility where I was teaching.

One asked me, "Do you ever see black dots in your eyes?"

I said, "Yes, I do. All the time."

She noticed that parts of my body were swollen and realized that something was wrong. She strongly suggested that my doctor check me out sooner rather than later.

Monthly appointments with my doctor were always a priority. I had a four o'clock visit scheduled that afternoon. When I arrived, the nurse took my blood pressure three or four times and then called in the doctor to take it. He asked me to give him my husband's number so he could call him. That was before the age of cell phones, so I gave him our home phone number.

I thought, *Why do you need to call him? I'm the one who's paying you.*

He recommended I check into the hospital for some rest. He wanted me to let my husband come and pick me up from his office, but I refused. He instructed me to report to the emergency room as soon as possible, saying they would admit me.

Being my usual self, I went home, washed clothes, straightened up the house, and took my time getting ready. When I arrived at the ER, the nurse said she had been waiting for me. She immediately had me sit in a wheelchair and began to literally run down the hall with me. Over my head was a sign that read "Intensive Care." I did not have any symptoms of illness or high blood pressure as far as I could tell.

The doctor did not want to alarm me by telling the real truth in his office. The nurses began to do tests and monitor my blood pressure. Another specialist who was covering for my doctor came in and said we would have the baby that evening. Talk about being shocked! I was only seven months pregnant.

My parents rushed to the hospital. My father was usually a very snappy dresser but not that night. He looked as if he had gotten dressed in the dark. He had on a checked shirt and pinstripe pants, which was never the way he dressed. I would have burst out in laughter if I had not been so terrified.

When the new doctor came in, he told me they would do an emergency cesarean section. We could not risk a normal delivery because of spiking blood pressure levels when contractions were induced.

Lamaze classes had been included in my pre-birthing plans even though I had my doubts about my ability to breathe right. When the doctor came in, we began to discuss my options.

"Just put me to sleep," I said. I was deathly afraid of getting a spinal.

After going back and forth, I guess he decided to shut me up and administered the anesthesia. He told me to count backward from one hundred. The Lamaze teacher later visited and jokingly told me that she thought I failed the course anyway.

Jonathan was born at nine thirty that evening. My husband's hand was bigger than he was. He weighed only two pounds and ten ounces at birth. His skin was so thin that we could see his veins, and his little feet were still turned inward.

Torrance later informed me that the doctor approached him and said there was a chance that one or both of us would not survive the delivery.

The doctor asked him, "If that becomes the case, should we save your wife or the baby?"

My husband told the doctor to save us both. God heard his prayer for our recovery. My seven-day stay in the hospital was on the maternity floor. While other mothers around me had their babies brought to them, Jonathan was housed in an incubator in the neonatology unit on another part of the hospital floor. This was very difficult for me to accept because I had gone to the doctor's appointments as scheduled, taken my vitamins, and did everything I could to have a healthy pregnancy.

Over the years I had talked to several teenage girls who boasted they had never seen a doctor or taken a supplement. After having been faithful to God, paying my tithes, and trying my best to live as God wanted me to, I questioned, "Why?"

My heart was broken because I could not hold my son. I could only touch him through the openings on the side of the incubator. He had to be exposed to light therapy for a lengthy period of time.

One of his pediatricians came into the room and saw me sobbing. She asked me directly why I was crying. I explained that the tears were because my baby was so ill.

She said something that has stayed with me since then. "You're always talking about your God. Don't you think that He will protect your baby?"

That was eye-opening. She made me think. This doctor was from another country, and I wasn't really sure what her religion was, but apparently I had impressed her with mine.

Prenatal classes only prepare mothers for full-term, healthy babies. The possibility that my son would not leave the hospital once I was discharged never entered my mind. He remained in their care for thirty-four days. Although the hospital staff urged me to stay at home and rest because of my surgery, I visited several times each day. He was so small and weak that he couldn't even cry out loud. To be sure that the nurses were taking proper care of him, I tried to sneak up on the floor. They did a wonderful job caring for him. It was just me being worried.

When it was almost time for his discharge, my husband's sister, Tommi, passed away in Chicago. She lost her battle with disease in less than three years. She was always active and a health nut for as long as I had known her. She pureed her vegetables and walked several miles a day before being stricken. After her first surgery, she walked the halls of the hospital to exercise. She too had so much to offer but was taken far too soon for anyone to comprehend. As a result my mother and father brought me home and stayed with me until my husband returned.

Jonathan is our miracle baby. He survived. Because he had been in an oxygen tank for an extended period of time, we had obvious concerns about his health. We took him to a number of specialists—optical, orthopedic, cardiac, and lung—to ensure he would develop normally. Because of God, Jonathan is healthy, brighter, and more intelligent than I could ever hope to be myself. Some may think that the age of miracles is over and that supernatural occurences ended with Jesus's physical presence on this earth. I beg to disagree. The day for miracles has not passed. My life and my success are both miracles. I am still looking for new wonders to arrive.

Jesus told His apostles in John 14:12–14, "Verily, verily, I say unto you, He that believeth on me, the works that I do shall he do also; and greater works than these shall he do; because I go unto my Father. And whatsoever ye shall ask in my name, that will I do, that the Father may be glorified in the Son. If ye shall ask any thing in my name, I will do it."

The high blood pressure diagnosed during my pregnancy never disappeared. Later I was misdiagnosed with lupus. A reaction to the medicine prescribed for the illness resulted in a hospital stay.

The doctor casually said, "Unfortunately you have lupus," just as easily as stating, "Have a nice day."

I had never heard of this disease or realized its gravity. When my levels seemed uncontrollable, I was referred for treatment to the Cleveland Clinic. Initially I was told that a helicopter would transport me. Since I wasn't sure that my insurance covered helicopter rides, I chose instead to drive the ninety miles to the facility. Miraculously a world-renowned specialist on autoimmune diseases was able to see me. He was consulting at the hospital with my doctor and asked if he could examine me. God placed him at the right place and time.

After an extensive examination and several blood tests, I was told to return within a week for the results of the checkup. The doctors established the true cause of my illness as rheumatoid arthritis, not lupus.

After those initial visits, my case was transferred to a rheumatologist in Youngstown. The medicines prescribed had many adverse side effects. I made appointments with an ophthalmologist every three months to ensure the medicine did not damage my vision and I had the ability to recognize color. Those visits continued for several years until the doctor determined that I no longer required treatment. God had performed another miracle in my life. The arthritis medicine was eliminated from my regimen.

Migraine headaches had also plagued me for years. They developed when I spent several hours a day looking at a computer screen as part of my job. At first they were tolerable, but they became more intense as the years passed. The pain and nausea became so severe that I would have to go to the emergency room for relief. I made an appointment with a physician who was knowledgeable regarding my recurrent illness.

During my first visit, he looked at the list of medicines I had been prescribed and asked, "Why are you taking this?"

I answered, "Because my former doctor ordered it."

He informed me that my high blood pressure medicine was not the most effective one for my ethnicity. Just as specific medicines produce better results on men than women, this one did not work as well on African Americans during drug trials. As a result he prescribed a different medicine. Within a month migraines no longer bothered me.

In doing further research, I discovered that a research team had studied this medicine and found it to be an agent of relief for those suffering with severe headaches. The high blood pressure was brought under control, and the headaches were eliminated as a bonus. God worked it out again through a great physician, to whom I will always be indebted.

God's promises for healing, prosperity, and success have been realized throughout my years. His promises are much more valuable because of His ability and willingness to see them come to fruition. By one person's count, there are 3,573 promises in the Bible. Among those assurances is that He would supply every need we have (Phil. 4:19), provide His grace through faith (2 Cor. 12:9), provide a way of escape so we need not be overtaken with temptation (1 Cor. 10:13), and find assurance in the knowledge that all things do work together for our good (Rom. 8:28).

God continues to answer my prayers at just the right time when I need a response or encouragement in a situation. He often reminds me when He fulfills a request that I placed before Him. On the evening before my graduation from Youngstown State University with my doctorate degree, my husband informed me that I had missed a phone call from one of my professors.

Immediately I panicked. Fears came to my mind that I had somehow failed to complete all my obligations and wasn't going to graduate. Hesitantly I returned the call. To my surprise, he asked if I would teach a course in the doctorate program the upcoming semester. God answered a prayer from 1971. He allowed me to teach on a university campus. He intervened and gave me not only a degree but unveiled the manifestation of a prayer.

That is why I encourage others to hold on to their dreams and hopes. Do not get tired and give up along the way. Those petitions have not been overlooked or gone unnoticed. God will reward you at just the right time and in the proper season.

Chapter 5:
THE INFLUENCE OF SPIRITUALITY AND FAITH ON EDUCATIONAL RESEARCH

So then faith cometh by hearing, and hearing by the word of God.
—Romans 10:17

Faith and spirituality have been sustaining forces in my life, as well as in the lives of others, to rise above circumstances and defeats. They are a part of my survival kit in a world filled with heartbreak and tragedy. Not a day can pass without reading or hearing about senseless killings and death. Homicide is the number-one cause of death for African American males between the ages of fifteen and thirty-four with 40 percent of all black men dying as a result of murder in 2011 (www.politifact.com/punditfact/statements/2014/aug/24/juan-williams).

Sadly my husband's son, Torrance Jr., was killed in our small town in 2001 at the tender age of thirty-three. He had been shot in the head for no discernible reason. Criminality touches each of us, no matter the race, religion, color, geographic location, or social or economic standing. No one lives outside of its reach. One could become a victim of crime while eating in a restaurant, sleeping soundly in his or her bed, riding on an airplane, or even shopping in the mall.

Recently nine people were viciously killed while attending Bible study in their house of worship in Charleston, South Carolina. The only safe place is in the arms of Jesus. There are those who suggest there is a correlation between crime and the lack of schooling. They surmise that students may resort to unlawful pursuits after realizing failure in school. These suppositions serve as further indictments on the nation's educational system and continue to be addressed.

Numerous studies have been conducted citing factors that attempt to explain the reasons why African Americans have not achieved their full potential in the workplace. The research frequently identifies the following as possible correlations to this current state of affairs: poverty, background, inequity, oppression, marginalization, lack of education or inferior schooling, homelessness, skills gap, low percentage of African American teachers, and exploitation. These factors do not exhaust the list of potential influences, but rather they enumerate those which are most familiar. Faith and spirituality, not only as they apply to my life, are examined in this chapter as to how others view their implications.

A body of literature exists that discusses spirituality as a factor that activates, transforms, and drives individuals. Historically the spirituality of African Americans has powered an inner strength, a source of human dignity, and a vehicle of hope for the future. It permitted African Americans to overcome racist and oppressive practices, and is a supportive force in the lives of many. Marable & Mullings (Garner 2002, 23) write, "Throughout the African American experience, spirituality has been a source for human renewal, survival, and resistance." Lives are connected to meaning and purpose through spirituality. It has been targeted as a key factor in the cultivation of academic and educational goals for numerous people.

Faith produces a reservoir of strength to rise above setbacks. It is important to recognize the spiritual energy that lies within each of us. Dantley (2005a, 655) credits spirituality for giving "people of color the impetus to create, innovate, and transform infirming and depreciating conditions," which they face throughout their life experiences. Garner (2002, 21) notes that spirituality encourages a "woman's sense of self, sense of mission and purpose in life, and the personal meaning that one makes out of one's work."

Dantley (2005a) describes spirituality as "a source of performative creativity in that it prods many African Americans to not only dream but also to strategize. Dreaming and visioning is a spiritual matter that demands courage and great faith. To dream is courageous enough, but to blend dreaming with an agenda of expected change moves into the realm of a kind of active or militant faith" (655).

Liebert and Dreitcher (1995, 39) further define spirituality as "the ongoing transformational experience of intentional, conscious engagement with the presence of God." Dantley (2005b) quotes Emmons (1999) in expressing spirituality as the following:

> A search for meaning, for unity and connectedness, for transcendence, and for the attainment of human beings highest potential. Spirituality is that realm of life that encompasses a set of principles and ethics to live by, commitment to God or higher power, recognition of the transcendent in everyday experience, a selfless focus, and a set of beliefs and practices that is designed to facilitate a relationship with this transcendent (502).

My faith in God and sense of spirituality guided the path that I followed in my career. As a student I was not fully aware of the numerous professional options available. I wrongfully assumed that my choices were limited. I also credit this lack of knowledge to the fact I was not exposed to people of color in challenging occupations. After a less than exhilarating experience touring a hospital and passing out at the sight of blood, I realized that nursing was not my forte. While I was in college, performing secretarial duties in a work-study job proved unfulfilling.

Requirements for a bachelor of science degree incorporated a mixture of courses. I enrolled in a history class that was really boring. The teacher never moved his mouth when he spoke. (I watched him.) Whenever I couldn't go to sleep, I would simply imagine myself in his class and would soon find myself knocked out. He was better than the sleeping pill Ambien. He could have been wealthy if he could have bottled that quality. History did not appear to be the field of study that gave me the most gratification.

My professional path was redirected after I enrolled in an African American history course. It was the first time that I had the opportunity to sit in a class with a black person teaching black history. Here was a professor with a PhD talking about critical historical events that had been either overlooked or eliminated from my past learning. I listened intently to every lecture and waited with great anticipation to attend those sessions. He enlightened the class on incidents that took place in the past, many of which had previously been disregarded and ignored in conventional classrooms. He didn't permit any fooling around and demanded that each student attend class daily and be punctual. Students admired this man, and I secretly coveted his ability to teach on that college campus.

One day in class, he turned to me and said, "Gaither, you need to teach."

I went to the registrar's office and changed my major that day. One person can have a profound effect on others' lives. This teacher cared about my future and perceived a gift within me. He identified my possibilities and potential because of his spirituality and my own. Greater things were in store for me. I can relate to Shirley Bynum's (2003, 47) encounter with her professor while in college. That professor helped her "realize that no matter who you are, if the determination and willpower is sufficient, you can make it." Because of Dr. Alex Farmer, I became a history teacher. This decision became the cornerstone of my future and career.

Before taking Dr. Farmer's class, I was unaware that teaching was one of the few career opportunities, historically, for women of color. Black men preached; black women taught. Black teachers, predominantly women, taught black children in segregated schools of the South. Teaching was one of the few professions open to black women since they were excluded from many professions open to men and available to white women. Black teachers in the segregated South could only teach in black schools. The numbers of white teachers increased with the onset of integration. White teachers in the North could teach black students.

With the advent of integration in the 1960s and 1970s, black students were transferred from black to white schools in the South. African American teachers and administrators who worked in black schools were not generally transferred to white schools. Consequently many black teachers lost their jobs during integration.

African American writers have inferred that black teachers in the segregated South fostered care and concern in their students. They were effective in that they listened to and understood their students. They knew the parents, lived in the same neighborhoods, and attended the same churches. Close relationships allowed teachers to have a better understanding of the children and their needs and backgrounds.

The black teachers in my father's segregated schoolhouse were stern disciplinarians. Dad attended a one-room schoolhouse that accommodated students from grades one through twelve. Teachers had the parents' permission to administer corporal punishment (spankings) to their children with the parents' blessing. Students knew, once they went home, they could expect more of the same. Kids would never indicate that the teacher was lying on them. That would bring even harsher consequences!

In my opinion a portion of the nurturing element has been lost in schools today. Changes occurred with the nation's dismissal of the religious component of education. Palmer (1993) insists there needs to be a spiritual dimension in teacher preparation. He regards spirituality as a human's yearning to be connected with something bigger than his or her own egos. He portrays education as a spiritual journey and notes that the inner lives of educators profoundly affect their profession. About his own life, he writes,

> My vocation is the spiritual life, the quest for God, which relies on the eye of the heart. My avocation is education, the quest for knowledge, which relies on the eye of the mind. I have seen life through both these eyes as long as I can remember—but the two images have not always coincided ... I have been forced to find ways for my eyes to work together, to find a common focus for my spirit-seeking heart and my knowledge-seeking

mind that embraces reality in all its amazing dimensions (xxiv).

The black church traditionally provided stability and leadership in the community. Religious denominations founded and funded early higher learning institutions for African American students. Adults in the black church could holler at, correct, and chastise children during services. Children were taught to behave in church. That pattern transcended the sanctuary and was reflected in the school.

When we were younger, we sat next to our mother in church. Dad was always in the pulpit. If I sat with the other children when I got older, I was expected to be attentive, listen to God's Word, and be an active participant in the worship service. My father would not hesitate to call out anyone if he or she were talking and not listening. No child wanted his or her parents to turn around in service and look at him or her. If my father did, I would just pray to God to take me now! If I weren't saved, I certainly gave an Academy Award-winning performance of a believer. I think the older people had eyes in the back of their heads. They knew what the young ones did wrong without looking. Most of the time, they were correct in their assumptions.

The Gaither children were taught to comport ourselves as ladies and gentlemen, no matter where we were. Our behavior was a direct reflection on our parents. Because we were preacher's kids, the pressure was even greater. I never remembered my father spanking the girls. Mother was the disciplinarian. The weeping willow trees in the yard were for more than just shade. My mother would always threaten us with, "Wait until your father gets home," which was enough to deter any misbehaviors. When he did come home, we pretended to be asleep.

My sister Judy and I attended a church service in her college town of Beaver Falls, Pennsylvania. The service seemed a little long, so I wrote her a note on the church bulletin asking how much longer it would last.

She replied, "When he closes his Bible, takes a few steps off of the pulpit, and walks into the audience, he will be done."

I replied, "Thank God."

I don't really know which of us left the bulletin on the pew of that church. By some strange coincidence, that same preacher was a guest speaker at our church a couple weeks later. Part of his remarks included reading the messages that my sister and I had sent to each other on his bulletin. If the floor had opened up, we would have sunk beneath it. My father gave us a very stern look and shook his finger at us. I still remember that expression.

Since I was a teacher in my hometown, the parents of my students were an extended family to me. It was commonplace for me to attend weddings, give eulogies at funerals, and shop in the same food markets. I can remember a parent approaching me while I was viewing a body at a funeral home. She did not hesitate to ask me about the detention I had assigned to her son, right there in front of the casket.

I actually started to shop outside of New Castle since it would take me two to three hours to get a few groceries because of all the conversation.

I was in a grocery store when a white woman came up to me and asked, "Are you a celebrity? Everyone seems to know you."

"In a small town," I explained, "everyone knows everyone, and usually knows everyone's business. Sometimes they simply make up what they don't know."

On another occasion a parent sought me out at our evening prayer meeting because her son had not come home from school. All night long I worried about that boy. Her son returned, but she never contacted me to tell me that he was safe. He and I had a long, up-front, and personal chat the next day in school. She didn't have that problem out of him again.

When a former student died unexpectedly, one of her relatives came to see me at my church. We talked about the mother's desire for her daughter to stay in school and graduate.

At the conclusion of our conversation, she asked, "Would you speak at her funeral?"

The answer was a resounding yes. The parent had worked hard in my high school class and had been determined to graduate. She envisioned the same outcome for her daughter.

At the funeral I reminded the girl of the last conversation I had with her mother. She had said, "I want her to graduate. End of story."

The mother and I talked about a variety of things on that day. I encouraged her to continue to attend church and instill her strong faith into her family. We also talked about possibilities. The now-grown adult admitted she hated school and would not want to attend any form of training in the future. The mother may not have always agreed with the advice given, but one would never know.

She would simply smile and say, "Yes, ma'am."

Bynum (2003, 47) writes that her black teachers made her feel valued and contends that the unconditional love and inspiration of spiritual black women makes the difference in the lives of black children. She found her way through obstacles and struggles by depending on her faith. She developed an inner strength that, in her words, "fueled my determination to succeed and discover that I was not inferior intellectually, culturally, or socially, but as smart and valuable as the next person."

For many, teaching is not simply a profession; rather it's an appointment or mission from God. It is an assignment with orders from above. If teaching is in someone, that person will teach, even if not in a formal setting. One can change location, but one can't lessen the desire to pursue teaching as a vocation if God has called them to do so. These teachers adhere to godly principles in their lives, which are reflected in their interactions with their students.

Hine and Thompson (1998, 123) conclude that "teaching was not simply employment for Black women—it was almost a holy calling, an opportunity for service to the race." Teaching is an opportunity to impart knowledge and impact the "whole" child. Walker (1996, 105) writes that "teaching was a worthy occupation and equivalent to a religious calling."

My summons into education came in a history classroom at the end of my sophomore year on the campus of Slippery Rock College. It became my mission to stimulate children's learning and excite them to find success in their lives. One can be born relatively poor, but poverty need not restrict achievement in an individual's life. We are all given certain opportunities, and it is our choice to take advantage of them as they present themselves. My work has not been in vain.

Faith and spirituality have fueled my drive and enabled me to maintain my focus. Hull (2001, 242) explains that "black people's spirituality—if acknowledged and consciously used—could be an awesome force" and it is "an untapped resource, a source of strength, and an important tool in the healing of African American women."

Stewart (1997, 20) remarked that "spirituality impacts the consciousness, identity, aspirations, and culture of African Americans and has been a principal catalyst in helping Black people maintain spiritual and social well-being despite their troubles." Faith and spirituality incorporate the basic theories of my theological foundation.

Chapter 6:
THE GROWING OF MY FAITH

For we walk by faith, not by sight.

—2 Corinthians 5:7

Delores Williams (1993, ix) writes, "Faith has taught me the gains, losses, stand-offs and victories in my life." College can be a scary place, especially if one has never lived long term away from home. Meeting new people with different backgrounds, religions, sexual orientations, and modes of thinking can be very intimidating to prospective students. I spent most of my time studying. As a result I missed a great deal of what some would call the college life. Attending a basketball or football game was never a priority.

We did have movie nights on campus. *Lady Sings the Blues* was one of my favorites. The school hosted *Roots* author, Alex Haley. What a charismatic storyteller he was! He shared detailed accounts of his numerous trips to Africa while researching his book, later to be made into a miniseries. The whole room was crying as he related encounters with his distant relatives. He sought a connection to his ancestry and found it.

Can you image going to college in 1971, right in the middle of the flower power days, without any jeans? My father said people wore blue jeans in the fields, so we never purchased any. For him jeans signified working, not fashion, statements. Not only that, we did not wear pants to school and work and certainly not church. Those were some very cold days walking across the campus unprotected! To this day I only own one pair of good jeans and still feel uncomfortable wearing them in public.

Slippery Rock, sometimes nicknamed "the slimy pebble," is a small, primarily white college located about twenty-five minutes from my hometown. There were few, if any, African Americans living in town, except for the college students and a few university employees. There were three or more black professors on campus during my stay. I had never seen the campus before I started classes. There was no such thing as a college tour, at least not for me. The application fee was fifteen dollars, and I only applied to one college. Basically whatever college I applied to, I had better been accepted to it. Black fraternities and sororities had not been established on the campus at that time either.

Attending a historically black college was out of the question because many of them were located in the South. That would make it more than thirty minutes from my home, my father's geographical requirement. Dad still had deep reservations about returning to the South on a permanent basis. The encounters of his past tarnished his memories. Reverend Gaither did not want any of his girls that far away.

A fair number of students were recruited from the Pittsburgh area to enhance the college's affirmative action agenda. Additionally Pennsylvania residents attended because state college tuition was more reasonable than a private college or university. It proved to be a solid educational foundation for me. I have never regretted my Slippery Rock days.

Upon viewing the campus that first day, I prayed and asked God to let me teach there one day. Almost forty years later, I received a call from the dean of the department of education, asking me to teach courses for the principal preparation program. I had to ask God for forgiveness. He remembered me; I had forgotten.

After three and a half years, I graduated from Slippery Rock State Teacher's College, now Slippery Rock University. I can remember entering college with the persistent thought, "Can I do this?"

I recently retrieved my college transcripts to apply for a new position in my now-retired life. I was pleasantly reminded that I did well in my undergraduate studies and extremely well in both graduate and doctorate programs.

You see, God does give us the desires of our heart. Our problem is time. We often think that prayers should be answered immediately. If they are not, we assume His answer is no. In this case the answer was to wait. It took precious time to prepare myself to be able to perform the duties of a professor, along with gathering the proper credentials.

Dr. Bernie Hoffman conducted numerous law seminars at the graduate level and coined the phrase, "in my certified, professional opinion." That phrase now reflects my qualifications and continues to speak volumes to my soul. There must be a season of preparation for the duties that lay ahead. Training is a prerequisite to fulfill one's destiny. The perfecting is in the process.

Once I graduated I assumed the doors of opportunity would immediately swing wide open. Many postulated that employment would be readily available. That isn't true. I can distinctly remember being refused applications for employment in several communities following my college graduation. Through persistence, determination, and divine intervention, I was able to begin the initial process. The acquisition of a position was not without effort.

After my hiring as an assistant principal, a white man in the grocery store asked, "What did they need: a black person or a woman?"

I said, "They needed someone with some sense because apparently you don't have any."

He, like many others, refused to acknowledge my years of study, training, knowledge base, and expertise in acquiring the position. I was well prepared to lead, but some relegated me to an affirmative action hiring.

As a black female educator, I was constantly charged with proving my worth. I worked harder and longer than many of my colleagues, often with little or no encouragement. The more I worked, the more I was required to work. I had to imitate King David of the Old Testament and encourage myself.

First Samuel 30:6 reveals, "And David was greatly distressed; for the people spoke of stoning him, because the soul of all the people was grieved, every man for his sons and daughters: but David encouraged himself in the Lord his God."

In spite of the outward tests, the strength to go on is hidden within each of us. If one is not familiar with David's situation, let me take a moment to paraphrase his story. The sworn enemy of the Israelites, the Amalekites, raided the city of Ziglag. The Amalekites knew that David and his army were away and the people of Ziglag could not put up a valid resistance against them. They raided the land and burned the city. The Amalekites also took the women captive, two of whom were David's wives.

When David and his six hundred men returned to the city, what he found horrified him. His men cried until they had no more tears left. The backlash of his soldiers was even more distressing. They blamed David and wanted to stone him because their family members had been kidnapped. Here was a man who had never lost a battle but was now the object of indictment by his people. There is no question that David faced trouble; the example is in how he prevailed. David believed in God and trusted in Him.

At this point David was alienated from his people, so he had to embolden himself. There are uncertainties in life. When all alone and those closest to you turn their backs and walk away, it is time to trust in the Lord.

As I continued to read 1 Samuel, I found that David depended on God to direct him in the fight against his adversaries. An Egyptian slave who was cast aside by his master informed David as to the location of the Amalekites' camp. David launched a surprise attack and killed all but four hundred of his opponents, "rescued all the people who had been kidnapped, and recovered all the belongings that had been taken from Ziglag" (Wiersbe 1982, 151).

I have included this account because I have found myself in predicaments that closely resemble David's story. No, I was not threatened with death, but people I respected turned against me when I attempted to do what I thought was right. At times I appeared to be alone, although many surrounded me. While counseling people, I point out that the sting of harsh words or pain of being stabbed in the back are not felt unless coming from those in close proximity. During these times dependence on God becomes amplified.

My faith has been tested on various occasions and through many situations. Through it all I learned to trust in God with more assurance. Shortly after I began my teaching career, I received a phone call from my sister Carmilla. She had gone into the doctor's office for a routine examination, and a small lump had been detected in her breast. She said not to worry, but that didn't ease my anxiety. When the lump was removed, the doctors discovered it was cancerous. Another call came in, and the family quickly left for Connecticut to be at her side.

We arrived after visiting hours. Dad was easily admitted because he had a clergy card. Mother was a missionary. No one would stop her either. Judy was seven months pregnant, and I was just me. Were we going to have a problem seeing my sister after traveling nearly ten hours? A kind security guard looked at us and beckoned for us to come in. For the next thirty days, I stayed in her home to help with her recovery and care for her daughter Akilah. She had faith that she would be healed completely from the cancer.

Chemotherapy and radiation treatments were prescribed. There were a few months of remission followed by recurrences of the disease in various parts of her body. Despite being treated by one of the finest hospitals in the country, a cure was not in her foreseeable future.

When Carmilla became too weak to care for herself and Akilah, she relocated to my home. She initially responded to treatment, but then her health began to fail again. Realizing that she might not live much longer, she asked if I would promise to raise her daughter. Doctors had advised her that the chances to prolong her life were nil if she did not undergo more chemotherapy. She rejected further treatment. I believe she was just sick and tired of being sick and tired.

An attorney came to my home, and we signed papers, giving me guardianship. Prayers went up to God for her healing. As the cancer metastasized, the pain often became unbearable, but she continued to trust God, and her faith did not falter.

Her complete healing came in another form. The Lord took her home to be with Him. Carmilla passed away on December 12, 1979. I believe that a portion of my father died with her. This was the daughter who had inherited his singing ability, a beautiful soprano voice. Church members often requested solos from her during services. She was the one who'd traveled with him in the evenings as he preached revival after revival. Carmilla was the really sweet one of the girls. She was my paternal grandmother's namesake and had died at a young age in her thirties, just as my grandmother had.

One of the condolences sent from a close friend remarked, "In the midst of her excruciating pain, her spirit remained unbroken as she was uplifted by her father's unabashed love for her."

I didn't know whether I would rebound from the loss of a sister. I was twenty-six years old, single, and now the mother to my niece. My prospective plans to attend law school seemed doubtful. It was another dream deferred. My sister had entrusted me with the care of her daughter. It was my duty not to fail her.

During the week that funeral arrangements were being made for Carmilla, I received some disturbing news of my own. A lump had been found in my left breast, but I had to wait until after the funeral to have it biopsied. I never told my parents. They were already in enough pain. A surgeon checked me again. The specialist said she was very confident that it was not malignant, but the procedure was performed as a precaution. The mass was benign, thank God. God gave me the strength to carry on.

My challenges came on both personal and professional levels. Being the only person of color in one's place of employment can be a formidable undertaking. Few, if any, opportunities arose to meet other African American teachers. On more than one occasion, I encountered white colleagues outside of school, and they ignored me. Other coworkers were open and invited me into their homes or to group gatherings.

The faculty frequently traveled to meetings in the tri-county area with similar demographics. In nearly all the conferences, I was the only African American teacher in the room. During the years I served as an administrator of the junior high school, four African Americans were on the faculty. Out of approximately a hundred teachers, two African Americans were on the faculty of the junior/senior high school. Although there was a high proportion of black students in the school, they did not see many people in authority or role models that looked like themselves.

Doughty (Jossey-Bass 1980, 239) writes that African American female administrators have to cope with the popular myth that black women are "superhuman, capable of solving any problem and dealing with any crisis, and stronger than other women and African-American men." Ortez (1982) and Korah (1990) report, "while women and minorities encounter barriers to leadership positions, minority women confront both gender and racial barriers" (Jossey-Bass 1980, 240).

White teachers would often ask me why all the black students sat together in the cafeteria. They said the black kids made the most noise. The white kids were sitting together too. Had they not noticed? In my home growing up and during Johnson family gatherings, the people who talked the loudest and fastest were the ones heard. We are a very vocal family. At times I still laugh, talk, sing, and praise loud, and it does not embarrass me. Proverbs 17:22 tells us, "A merry heart doeth good like medicine." In some scenarios you have to laugh to keep from crying.

In times of distress, I looked toward heaven. Psalm 121:1–2 encouraged me to "lift up mine eyes unto the hills, from whence cometh my help. My help cometh from the Lord, which made heaven and earth."

Take my advice. Trust God.

Chapter 7:

THE BENEFITS OF BEING FAITHFUL

A faithful man shall abound with blessings.
—Proverbs 28:20

Psalm 116:12 asks, "What shall I render unto the Lord for all his benefits toward me?" In that stead, believers acknowledge that God has conferred certain rewards and benefits to those who remain faithful, dedicated, and committed. To be faithful indicates that one is systematic, methodical, and thorough in the performance of duties; true to his or her word, promises, and vows; and steady in allegiance or affection to God. Faithfulness also suggests reliability and trustworthiness in fulfilling obligations (Merriam-Webster).

Perhaps the most valuable aspect of this attribute is the fact that the faithful will not suffer God's judgment. But until our Judgment Day, we can receive some benefits while here on earth.

- "For the Lord loves the just and will not forsake his faithful ones" (Ps. 37:28).
- "My son, do not forget my teaching, but keep my commands in your heart, for they will prolong your life many years and bring your prosperity" (Prov. 3:12).

- "Through love and faithfulness sin is atoned for; through the fear of the Lord a man avoids evil. When a man's ways are pleasing to the Lord, he makes even his enemies live at peace with him" (Prov. 16:6–7).

One of the most important components of Christian life should be faithfulness to God. Truthfully adherence to almighty God is the only thing we can count on. I believe it is important to share a few of the difficulties as well as the triumphs of my life—all of which I credit to my faithfulness to God—which I rightly regard as the benefits of being faithful.

As previously stated my first professional assignment was as a history teacher. I definitely needed determination and persistence to obtain an application for employment. At first I was told that no positions were available, even though the newspaper had posted the resignation of a history teacher. Contact with the National Association for the Advancement of Colored People (NAACP) and the Equal Employment Opportunity Commission (EEOC) enabled me to secure the paperwork. Because I never knew if I would need those agencies again, I kept the phone numbers nearby for quick access.

Once the interview process took place, a job offer was presented. Because I was the last to be hired, there was always the possibility that I would be the first to be laid off. I taught a variety of courses at the school and, over time, found my niche teaching at-risk students. I was also elevated to a coordinator position, which included recruiting students for enrollment.

As a result I traveled to schools in Lawrence County and presented materials regarding the opportunities afforded to those who acquired marketable skills while in high school. I approached a biracial student in one of the classes. A look of fear came over his face as I attempted to talk to him. I believe that this was his first encounter with an African American. His reservations were calmed for the moment, but I always wondered how he adjusted in the real world filled with diversity.

Because of my recruitment duties, my teaching time was reduced. The at-risk classes were scheduled in coordination with my additional responsibilities. Many of the students were placed with me because of their actions in previous classroom settings. Somehow their behaviors changed for the better with our meeting. They knew I would sternly reprimand them or reward them with praise, as the situation required. The students demonstrated openness to my old-school teaching techniques and an appreciation for the opportunity to grow academically.

Each week the class was rewarded with treats if everyone attended daily. For me both intrinsic and extrinsic rewards provided significant motivators for students. They put pressure on each other to attend. Certificates were awarded every nine weeks to those who worked the hardest. The honors were not always bestowed on those with the highest grades. The amount of effort given was the quality being recognized.

Once during a fire drill, a few of my students escaped from my view. They returned a few minutes later with a handful of live flowers and presented them to me. I found out that they had picked them from a nearby home during the drill. It was a beautiful thought but just handled the wrong way. After contacting the homeowner, my students and I planted new flowers in his yard the next week.

Throughout my teaching career, the enhancement of the learning culture was my objective. I designed activities to uncover positive high school experiences. Surprisingly some of the students had never been outside of the city limits. A trip to Youngstown, Ohio, seemed commonplace to me. That was my route to work each day. Several students had never been to nearby amusement parks or shopped in the Southern Park Mall in the suburbs of Youngstown. Some families did not own cars and had no vehicles for travel.

My heart was pricked. How often did I take my good fortune for granted? We raised funds to take some of the young people to dinners and class trips to parks, museums, art galleries, and zoos. Students were taken to eat in restaurants too. On one trip we went to a restaurant whose title included the words "Restaurant and Saloon," a Texas-style steakhouse.

One of the girls asked, "Do they do hair here too?"

Get it? Salon? Saloon. I still smile about that one.

After several years of teaching, I was informed that I would be laid off the following school year. One position had to be eliminated because of a decline in enrollment. Some advised me to take the layoff. Those words came easily from their mouths. They had secure positions. It was not as easy for me to accept. After calling the NAACP office, recommendations were given as to the actions I should take. God stepped in. His spirit was leading me; my response was by faith.

I heard His voice as clear as if I were talking to another person. The voice said, "Call the Department of Education."

I must say that my faith at the time was still a work in progress. After speaking to numerous people, the general consensus was that no one could help me. Finally during the last transfer of my call, a voice came on the phone. I told him my name and explained my situation.

He said, "Repeat your name and spell it for me." I complied with his request.

He then remarked, "That's funny. I am looking at your name on a form in front of me. Someone has nominated you as Pennsylvania Teacher of the Year, and all applications are forwarded to me."

He asked, "How can one of the best teachers face layoff?"

He informed me that he needed fifteen minutes to resolve my predicament. He called back to assure me that I would be working the next year.

I met that representative years later at a NAACP banquet. He remembered me and asked how I was doing. Because of his involvement, I could truthfully respond that I was fine. I was able to thank him in person for his intervention on my behalf. Yes, that is how God works, in unforeseen ways and through unexpected people.

My sister Judy taught elementary school for ten years and then followed God's guidance to leave her job and pursue a doctorate in educational administration at Miami University of Ohio. Dr. Judy Gaither McConnell-Jackson was killed in a collision on November 6, 1992, after an oncoming truck struck her vehicle. The accident occurred while she was in Tampa, Florida, recruiting minority students for graduate studies.

When the family initially received the phone call from the hospital about the accident, it seemed like a nightmare. We prayed that her injuries were superficial. We learned she had been ejected on impact from the convertible she was driving. I went to my bank to get money to travel to Florida. The call came back to say that she had passed away from internal injuries. Her husband was flying to Florida to surprise her. He instead had to escort her body home.

My parents were devastated with the loss of not one but two daughters. It is every parent's nightmare to bury a child. Each was talented in her own right; both had the capacity to make significant contributions to society. Judy's sixteen-year-old son was with her in Tampa but had waited in the hotel for her return from the presentation. Fortunately a few of her colleagues knew he was there and looked after him until his stepfather arrived.

Judy had always vowed that she did not want to outlive my father. Her affirmation came true. Miami University held several memorials in celebration of her life. Hundreds attended a gospel concert in her honor. Over a thousand people came through the line the next night to view her body and mourn her loss. The eulogy was entitled "Sunset at Noon."

The message was taken from Romans 8:28. "And we know that all things work together for good to them that love God, to them who are called according to his purpose." The pastor spoke about how things have no feelings but still have a function as they work within God's design.

Judy called me a few weeks before her death, and she was so excited about the scripture from Jeremiah 29:11. "For I know the plans I have for you, declares the LORD, plans to prosper you and not to harm you, plans to give you hope and a future." She was convinced that her future was in the hands of God. Little did I know that those words would be repeated at her home-going service.

The speaker enumerated the many accomplishments that Judy made during her forty-two years on earth. She lived a very full life. She traveled, shopped, bought great cars, and enjoyed the amenities of life. Some people could live a century and never have been as productive as she was.

We held a second service in New Castle. We borrowed a church to hold the crowd. People came from all over the United States to attend. The numerous accolades, tributes, and flowers acknowledged one who had successfully completed life's race. She now rests beside my parents, sister, grandparents, and uncle. A portion of my extended family is buried behind their graves. My family reunions are held in Graceland Cemetery, but I can only hold a one-way conversation.

Her death came one month before I received my principal's certificate. She had planned a graduation party for me but didn't live to see me receive the degree. Every time I saw her former principal after that, he mistakenly called me by her name and then began to cry.

My parents and I shared the raising of her son. He was in tenth grade when he relocated to New Castle. Because he had been schooled in a college town, we looked for an equivalent curriculum that included the study of Latin. Only one school in the vicinity offered this course. He was enrolled in Catholic education. That meant I came to my parents' home a half hour earlier each morning to take him to his bus stop. Sometimes I didn't get home until eight or nine o'clock in the evening, only to begin the routine the next morning. My parents had suffered the loss of their daughters, and I wanted them to be close to their grandchildren. That was the least I could do.

God continued to control my destiny. One day I had a chance encounter with a local official, who remarked, "I heard you have a principal's certificate. Why don't you apply for New Castle's current opening?"

I thought about it for a minute and then pondered, *Why not apply? All they can say is no.*

He made no promises that I would be awarded the job, only saying he would mention my name as a candidate for an interview. The rest would be up to me. I completed the application but had serious doubts about my ability to obtain the position. Oftentimes in school communities, hiring is done on the basis of who you know, not particularly what you know. I was not related to anyone with sway and not connected politically. My advantage was that I knew God and He had a plan for my life.

After participating in an extensive interview in July, the district did not follow up with me.

They had asked, "If you could build a collage of yourself, what would it include?"

I answered that it would be fourfold. First there would be a picture of my church, followed by a picture of my family, an image of a school, and end with a photograph of Saks Fifth Avenue. They all chuckled, but truthfully those were my four great loves. I have since divorced Saks and replaced it with Neiman Marcus.

The plan was to return to my classroom in September and be grateful for my current position. On the evening of the first day of the new school year, I received a call offering me the job, starting the next day. How could I leave my job without a two-week notice?

The caller informed me that it would be taken care of. God worked in and through that gentleman, and I am thankful for that.

My new position was as the assistant principal of both the junior and senior high schools. They were located on separate campuses, so a bit of travel was required. Handling discipline was my primary responsibility. I have always worn high heels, and the students got used to hearing the clicking of my shoes as I approached. The newspaper once interviewed a student, and he noted that students moved when they heard the heels coming. The sound reminded them to discontinue anything they had no business doing. It was my gentle hint to get to steppin'.

Although another African American female principal was in the school district, researchers indicate that women and people of color are underrepresented in educational leadership positions in schools. It is even more difficult to attain employment as a principal at the secondary school level.

Eden (1987) interviewed female administrative aspirants in his study, and most agreed "they had to be far superior to male candidates just to be considered for an administrative position and, even then, school boards still showed a preference for hiring men" (Jossey-Bass 1980, 223). Cantor (1977) argued that three dynamics may result when there are small numbers of women within these ranks:

a) Women in those positions may receive more attention.
b) The additional attention may lead to more pressure to perform.
c) The organization's cultural boundaries may be heightened to polarize and exaggerate the differences between males and females. (Jossey-Bass 2000, 227)

One of the benefits of being faithful was that God gave me acumen, the ability to make good judgments and quick decisions, as the principal of the junior high school. As high stakes testing became a prominent fixture in school agendas, my goal was to seek out and improve the test scores of minority students in the district. During my term as a junior high principal, I wrote and copyrighted a pilot middle school motivational program for students of color entitled "Children of Promise." Children of Promise is a faith-based initiative that proposes an investment in the educational futures of children. The program outlined a fivefold approach to student success and achievement based on Philippians 4:13, "I can do all things through Christ."

Inspiration for Children of Promise came as a result of the 2001 national educational initiative, No Child Left Behind (NCLB). A sense of urgency was evident after reviewing the provisions of the law. NCLB was an update of the Elementary and Secondary Act of 1965. It was prompted by the nation's report card, the study from the National Assessment of Educational Progress (NAEP). The results consistently reflected a four-year skills gap between black and white students. It was determined that Hispanics were not doing much better.

NCLB required all students to perform at proficient or advanced levels in reading and math by the year 2014. Specific subgroups (forty students or more) within the school population were delineated and targeted by federal and state law for marked improvement. African American students in Ben Franklin met the prerequisites to be designated as a subgroup.

Children of Promise sought out hardworking eighth-grade students who were high performing, and self-motivated. It was designed to push students to new academic heights by exposing them to civic, social, and educational arenas. Children of Promise addressed students who could be propelled to higher levels of scholastic success. Students were challenged to complete the following goals throughout the remainder of their years in school:

(1) Model positive behavior to peers and family
(2) Attend school regularly and be punctual
(3) Improve grades and enroll in accelerated college-bound courses
(4) Score at the advanced level on state-sponsored testing
(5) Be enrolled in a college or school for advanced training in five years

The five components of the Children of Promise are spirituality, family, education, socialization, and community service.

SPIRITUALITY

Spirituality can be the impetus needed to push people forward. It provides a means of self-actuation and survival; it is a sustaining force in the lives of many African Americans. Spirituality is a source of strength used to rise above situations and shortcomings. It is the root of the Christian faith, no matter the denomination. Once appropriately recognized spirituality can be a formidable addition to personal energy. The fact that research recognizes the importance of spirituality is compelling in itself. Spirituality takes us further into our beliefs. Dantley (2005b) eloquently explains the power of spirituality:

> [It] enables us to connect with other human beings; it underpins our ability to dismantle marginalizing conditions while simultaneously creating strategies to bring about radical changes in less-than-favorable circumstances. Our spirituality is the core of who we are. Our spirituality connects our lives to meaning and purpose. (654)

FAMILY

The family is the cornerstone of our natural support system. It is often said, "Blood is thicker than water" and "The family that prays together stays together." The world in which we live does not always portray families in the traditional sense. The dynamics of families and living arrangements have changed over time. According to a study by Vespa, Lewis, and Kreider (2013), 55 percent of black children and 31 percent of Hispanic children were more likely to live with one parent than non-Hispanic or Asian children. A mother who is either the sole or primary breadwinner of the family heads four in ten American households with children under the age of eighteen.

The report also concluded that there was a dramatic increase in the numbers of single-parent families in the United States over the last thirty years. In 1970, a single parent headed 13 percent of families.

One-fourth of the children in the United States lived with a single parent in 1996. Women headed approximately 84 percent of these families in 2012. Divorced or separated mothers were the head of household in 58 percent of those surveyed; 24 percent of mothers were never married. Other family heads included the following: widows (7 percent), divorced and separated fathers (8.4 percent), never-married fathers (1.5 percent), and widowers (0.9 percent). There is disparity in the numbers of families headed by a single parent by ethnicity; 22 percent are white, 57 percent are black, and 33 percent are Hispanic.

In the past, single-parent families were the result of parental death. About one-fourth of children born around the turn of the nineteenth century experienced the loss of a parent before they reached age fifteen. The factors most commonly related to the contemporary American single-parent family are changing social and cultural trends, increased rates of divorce, nonmarital childbearing, increased employment opportunities for women, decreased employment opportunities for men (especially African American men), and availability of welfare benefits that enable women to set up their own households (Rodgers 1996). It has been estimated that half of the babies born in the United States will spend some part of their childhood with a single parent as a result of separation, divorce, or out-of-marriage births.

Michael Fullan (Blankstein 2004, 167) asserts, "The research is abundantly clear: Nothing motivates a child more than when learning is valued by schools and families/communities working together in partnership. These forms of involvement do not happen by accident or even by invitation. They happen by explicit strategic intervention."

Further, the research of Henderson (1987) and Henderson and Berla (1995) concludes that "greater parental involvement leads to greater student achievement, irrespective of such factors as socioeconomic status or ethnic background" (Blankstein 2004, 168).

Despite the changes we see in society, Christians cannot vacillate in their commitments. The obligations to families extend far beyond the bloodline. We are our brother's keeper. Bynum (2003, 137) writes that black women understand "the importance of education in the success of community and dedicated their lives to the uplift of the race, by reaching back to pull up the children."

Without my family I would not have had the courage to dream nor the energy to chase my aspirations.

EDUCATION

Early in my life, I was taught that education was the key to success. Be that as it may, without using the key in the door of opportunity, we remain locked out, shut out, left out, and less than marketable in the workforce. Education produces unmistakable opportunities for advancement. Taking advantage of these prospects has not always been fully realized. A careful examination of history enables one to recognize and appreciate the sacrifices made for African Americans to be educated.

The sufferings of our predecessors to guarantee the availability of education should never be minimized or forgotten. Oftentimes specifics of that hard-fought struggle have not been passed down to children. It is not enough to pay homage on Martin Luther King Jr. Day only. Someone once said, if we forget our history, we are destined to repeat it. I saw a billboard that pictured children in a classroom. The caption read, "You never know who might be in the class: a doctor, a lawyer, or another Martin Luther King Jr."

Every educational opportunity should be savored. Every learning experience must be cherished. Every child should be urged to reach his or her full potential and not squander his or her time, talents, and gifts.

During slavery it was against the law to teach black children to read. Slavery denied the opportunity for a formal education to these individuals. Painter points out (2006, 133) that blacks had been "kept uneducated, and they rightly regarded their ignorance as a badge of servitude." Thernstrom and Thernstrom (2003, 121) further explain that slaves were "denied the opportunity to learn to read and write; even a little learning might have inspired a dangerous thirst for freedom." Gates (1987) noted that the slave who was the first to read and write was the first to run away. There was a definite correlation between literacy and freedom.

The Supreme Court ruling in *Plessy v. Ferguson* (1895) established the principle that public facilities, including schools, could legally be separate but equal. Homer Plessy had challenged the Louisiana law that required the railroad to segregate blacks and whites on trains in the state. The Supreme Court ruled that a separate car did not violate Plessy's rights because he was allowed to ride on the train. The ruling legalized segregation and noted that enforced separation of the races did not signify inferiority. States could now legally establish separate systems of education and require that division as well.

Inferior books and supplies, inadequate facilities, insufficient funding of schools and teachers, and lack of bus transportation characterized public education for African Americans during the period of legalized segregation. Teacher training was restricted for black educators due to limited number of institutions of higher learning. Students who wanted more than an elementary education during segregation often left the South in order to attain these goals. *Plessy v. Ferguson* was eventually overturned in the landmark decision, *Brown v. the Board of Topeka, Kansas* (1954), when attorneys successfully argued that segregated schools were inherently unequal.

By a unanimous vote, the justices of the Supreme Court ruled that segregation deprived African American children of their right to equal protection, as the Fourteenth Amendment guaranteed. The Supreme Court agreed with the facts presented by a team of NAACP attorneys headed by Thurgood Marshall. The decision was a triumph for African Americans because it destroyed the constitutional foundation on which the concept of segregation had been built.

The establishment of Jim Crow laws and ordinances in the 1870s created a caste system in the United States that regulated the status of African Americans' social, political, and economic life. The statutes enforced underlying racial issues until the Civil Rights Movement of the 1960s brought an end to these practices by exposing America's shameful conduct and by pursuing legal recourse. West (1999, 101) affirms, despite the challenges of segregation and discrimination, "African Americans had the dogged determination to survive, the tenacious will to persevere, persist, and even prevail against the unrelenting assault on Black humanity."

Students of color often fall short on levels of achievement, some of which is by design. Our forefathers went above and beyond the call of duty to ensure that civil rights were extended to all citizens. The risk of imprisonment, beatings, and death did not impede that struggle. The dangers they faced should be honored by our vigor to do more, learn more, earn more, and always vote.

President John F. Kennedy stated, "Let us think of education as a means of developing our greatest abilities, because in each of us there is a private hope and dream which, fulfilled, can be translated into benefit for everyone and greater strength for our nation" (Howe 2003, 28).

Thernstrom and Thernstrom (2003) furnish evidence that a great skills gap exists between black and white students. According to their research, an equal number of years spent in school does not certify that students receive an equal education or that equal knowledge is acquired. As a result there are increased numbers of unemployed people of color and an underrepresentation of blacks in positions of educational leadership, power, and influence.

Jacqueline Jackson further notes that black women are "the poorest of the poor, and the most oppressed of the oppressed" (Hull 2001, 146). She further submits that this claim can be substantiated by the fact that black women are the most disadvantaged group in the United States, as "evidenced by their largely unenviable educational, occupational, employment and income levels, and availability of marital partners."

Carlson (1998, 197) correlates spirituality and an individual's perspective of education. He notes, "Education is, in the fullest sense, a spiritual experience. It changes the way we experience our being in the world, it reconnects us to the cosmos and its transforms us in ways that affect our everyday relations with others and makes it possible for us to struggle and grow."

A minimum of a high school diploma is essential. An African proverb discloses, "Not to know is bad; not to wish to know is worse" (Howe 2003, 21). Over the course of a lifetime, adults with an inferior education will earn less money. It has been observed that those who do not make it through high school have a far greater risk of incarceration and drug abuse than their peers do.

Education pays off in the long run. With increased levels of schooling comes a greater expectation of earning power. According to data obtained through Current Population Source and quoted in research by Thernstrom and Thernstrom (2003, 37), students who "left school before ninth grade earn only a third as much as those who completed a bachelor's degree."

I must admit that I have encountered a few young people who only wanted to stay in school long enough to be able to sign for their government assistance check. These were not African Americans for the most part; rather they were white students who had become encapsulated in the system. It is up to schools to change the mind-set of anyone who has developed this mode of thinking.

Not only is it incumbent on schools to provide an equal education, they must also furnish an equivalent opportunity for success. When talking with people about their life plans, I often ask where they hope to be in the next five to ten years. Perhaps the most troubling answer begins with the words, "I'm about to …"

For me, that signals no clear strategy or focus. When I asked again the next year, no steps had been taken. I believe that a person can only expect failure if a life plan has not been developed. In the words of a very wise man (my father), it is time to "bale up that hay," the advice he gave an extremely long-winded preacher whose sermon went from the books of Genesis to the Revelation inclusively.

The sense of urgency to develop career goals among young people was an impetus in the foundation of Children of Promise. The plan included scheduling courses in high school that coincided with their future designs. Until that occurs many will find themselves in the same predicament years later, wondering where the time went.

Bringing together a precise course of action makes the process easier. My advice is to stop making excuses about the inability to secure an education. There are enough grants, loans, and subsidies available to ensure that anyone can enroll in some type of training. Students have access to both short- and long-term programs and should not prejudge postsecondary experiences by those faced in high school. My counsel is to, once started, stick with their education.

One young man told me, "If God wills, I will go to college."

I told him God already "wills" him to go to college. God told us in His Word "to study to show ourselves approved" (2 Tim. 2:15). Stop worrying God about the good that He has already planned. Ask to be led in the right direction and then just do it.

SOCIALIZATION

Today's students should be exposed to various cultural, educational, and social arenas. Education goes beyond the borders of brick and mortar. For many years I encouraged my staff to plan field trips and incorporate outdoor and critical thinking activities into lesson plans. If students are allowed to see more, they yearn for more.

One of the projects for the Children of Promise program was to take students on tours of college campuses. They visited the libraries, ate in the cafeterias, perused the dorms, and more. For some these excursions provided a first opportunity to walk on a college campus. My thinking was to eliminate the fear of going to college by showing that there was nothing to fear. President Franklin D. Roosevelt expressed it best when he declared during his 1933 Inaugural Address, "The only thing we have to fear is fear itself" (Rosenman 1938, 11). If we excite students about college, they will be more inclined to attend a postsecondary institution.

Our culminating activity for the Children of Promise was a trip to Washington, DC. It was an exhilarating time for all of us. Students and parents raised money for the trip. We were also given financial assistance from the school district, local churches, and individual benefactors who heard about our project. I had not visited the monuments and official destinations since I was in sixth grade. Many students had never spent a night in a hotel. That was truly exciting!

We sat and watched the changing of the guards at Arlington National Cemetery. We were led to the gravesite of President Kennedy and his family. We viewed the grave of boxer Joe Louis, who is related to my cousins by blood. We visited the home of Frederick Douglass's birth. We walked the halls of the National Archives Museum and ate in the huge food court in the Ronald Reagan Building and International Trade Center.

We scanned the Vietnam Wall and searched for the name of George Threats, one of my husband's best friends and the first African American to die in the Vietnam War from our hometown. The steps to the Lincoln Monument were formidable after a long day of sightseeing, but we climbed anyway. We visited the African American Museum of Art and later ate at Ben's Chili Bowl, a business owned and operated by a black man with an entire African American staff. Many students had never witnessed this before. Ben's exposed them to the possibility of becoming entrepreneurs.

Mr. James O. Payne, a teacher who said the "O" stood for "outstanding," came along to help supervise the male students. He had spent his summers in Washington, DC, and knew the District well.

We stood outside the White House in awe, never knowing that a man of color would inhabit it one day for two terms of service. We briefly observed the campus of Howard University, a historically black university that Oliver O. Howard founded in Washington, DC, in 1867. Students were previously instructed to keep some of their spending money. A souvenir from Howard University was a must.

This was an experience I would never forget, and I suspect neither will the members of Children of Promise. The trips proved to be a catalyst that heightened student awareness and impacted thought processes. The experiences permitted young people to channel goals into reality. Parents and former students still extend their appreciation to me for this aspect of the program. I believe Children of Promise had a profound effect on every participant.

COMMUNITY SERVICE

Community service is giving back and putting words into action. Every deed is valuable when performed in the right spirit. This tenet is one of the beliefs central to the Christian faith. Yes, it is better to give than to receive (Acts 20:35). We are blessed when we extend our time, energies, and gifts to others.

Values are gained when pupils become involved in community service. Students who participate in community service

a) tend to do better academically in school by applying what they have learned in the classroom to real human needs;
b) recognize that they can actually make a difference with what they do and better understand their own competence and an increased sense of self-efficacy (community service leads to more self-confidence in their work and academic pursuits);

c) learn how to problem solve and overcome hurdles they may face in their own lives;
d) find a sense of responsibility and pride; and
e) learn how to work better in teams. (www.college.org/2012/06/27/12-reasons-community-service-should-be-required)

Although the pilot group consisted of thirty-five students, my goal was for full participation for every student of color. I hoped students would transform their views on achievement. Jabez prayed to God in 1 Chronicles 4:10, "Oh, that thou would bless me indeed, and enlarge my coast and that thine hand might be with me …"

God heard his prayer, and the Bible notes that God granted him all he requested. God continues to hear and answer prayers, and He provides every good and perfect gift. That is why I pray the Jabez Prayer often.

The New Testament confirms the ability to have needs fulfilled. The Lord has promised in Matthew 7:7–8, "Ask, and it will be given to you; seek, and you will find; knock, and it will be opened to you. For everyone who asked receives, and he who seeks finds, and to him who knocks will be open."

I heard a story once about a frog, although I am not sure who to credit it to and I may have adjusted it quite a bit to fit my needs. It illustrates the benefits of being persistent in establishing one's goals. This is how I tell it.

> Several frogs were in a barrel. One tried to escape by leaping out. The other frogs mocked him. One told him that he was too dumb to get out of the barrel. Another told him he wouldn't get out of the barrel because he was too poor. Lighter-skinned frogs told him that he was destined to live in the barrel because he was darker than the other frogs. Some had the audacity to tell him that he was from the wrong side of the barrel. Still the frog continued to leap until he jumped out of the barrel. The unknown truth of the story is that the frog was deaf. He couldn't hear the negatives. He didn't know

he had those factors going against him, and he got out anyway! The now-liberated frog never heard the pronouncements on his life for failure or remaining in the same state he was in.

There is a message in this story: concentrate on the positive, pretend you don't hear the naysayers, ignore the haters, and keep leaping toward your goal.

Chapter 8:
THE STORIES YOU MAY NOT BELIEVE

There is nothing so strange and so unbelievable that it has not been said by one philosopher or another.

—Rene Descartes (www.brainyquote.com/quotes/authors/r/rene_descartes.html)

Often I sit back and laugh remembering the many humorous events that occurred when I was a teacher and principal. Other encounters bring great sadness to my heart. I want to relate a few of the stories because, even in dark situations, God brought peace to my soul. They are told in no particular chronological order. Each has its own meaning for me, which I believe is worthy of sharing.

I am the first to admit that I would sometimes address a student as "my child" or "baby." Not only were they terms of endearment, it was also a way for pupils not to notice that I was not at all good at remembering names. Throughout my career I have worked with thousands of students. My memory has failed me from time to time. The same could be said of my former students.

While riding the escalator in a department store one day, I noticed a man staring at me. I could see from the look on his face that he recognized me, probably as the only African American teacher in his life.

He smiled and said, "Hi, Mrs. Black."

I didn't correct him. As least he acknowledged me.

While rehearsing for commencement one year, I called the name of one of the students to cross the stage. She shyly corrected my pronunciation.

I asked her, "How do you pronounce your name?"

Graduation was a memorable event in the students' lives, and I wanted to make sure I gave each the proper recognition for the occasion. To be sure I was totally correct, I asked again and even wrote it out phonetically as a backup.

After practice I spoke to the girl. I had taught her mother, I was at the hospital shortly after this girl's birth, and I had watched her grow throughout her childhood.

I asked, "What have I been calling you all these years?"

She responded, "Baby."

Just before dismissal a school administrator called me to his office. When I arrived a male student was seated in front of his desk. Both had tears in their eyes. His parents had put this young man out of his home. After confirming that his story was true, we began to discuss options for the student. It was not my intent to judge his parents; rather I was to assist this student.

After speaking to the boy, I found out that he had relatives living about sixty miles from my residence. A person who was always impeccably dressed now looked disheveled and smelled of mothballs. A phone call was placed to his extended family to explain the dilemma. We secured his belongings, and he went to live with them. Now whenever I see this man, he thanks me for intervening in his life. His pain was obvious. I found new respect for my administrator that day too.

One of my students returned to my classroom after dismissal while I was still working at my desk. He came back to tell me that he had nowhere to go. His mother had moved out of town while he was in school that day and never told him where she was going or said she had planned to move. It took some time and assistance from community resources, but we found him a place to live, and he was able to graduate.

Having an open-door policy for faculty, staff, students, and parents proved to be beneficial. My secretary called my office phone to inform me that two young ladies were waiting to talk to me. I told her to let the assistant principal handle it because I was involved in a lengthy conference. She said they wanted to wait for me.

After concluding my session, I invited the girls in and asked, "Why didn't you want to talk to my assistant?"

One of the girls told me that someone had done something wrong to them. She wanted me "to cuss him out."

I told her, "You know I don't cuss."

She said, "Yeah, but he'll wish you did when you get through with him."

After listening to their complaints, I discovered that a visiting college recruiter had made unwanted advances, calling and texting the girls using phone numbers listed on official documents. He wanted to meet outside of school hours and asked inappropriate personal questions of them. His behavior would not go without report or reprimand.

I was on the phone immediately with the college, the recruiter's supervisor, parents of the students, and the recruiter himself. Afterword a formal complaint was filed, and the university assured me that he would no longer work at the college.

The well-being of students was always a priority. If a student became severely ill during school hours and an ambulance was called, my nurse or I would accompany the student to the hospital and remain there until a parent arrived. When one boy was injured in a car accident on the way to school, my first response was to go to the hospital. The boy told his mother that he was surprised that I came to see about him.

I said, "Be surprised if I don't."

Appearances in courtrooms were listed among my duties as principal. During a hearing I sat near the rear of the courtroom as the officer escorted a former student into the proceedings. The man's mother was clearly upset with him. He had started a disturbance, and I had witnessed the ruckus.

The mother looked at him disgustedly and said out loud, "I told you not to (expletive) with Dr. Respress."

It took several minutes before the courtroom regained composure.

I once called a home to speak with the parents of a boy who had violated school policy. No one answered the phone, but a message came on from the father. He said, "You have reached my (expletive) house, and I am too (expletive) busy to answer, so leave me a (expletive) message."

What then can you expect from the children?

One of my female students held a very special place in my heart. She became ill and had been taken to the hospital for emergency surgery. The hospital called and informed me that she would not consent to the surgery unless I was there. I left my office and went to the hospital. When I arrived she was on the gurney and asked me to pray for her. I told her that I was her principal and not allowed to pray for her because of the separation of church and state.

She looked at me lovingly and said, "You're not my principal here."

I responded, "Our Father, who art in heaven …"

A senior class trip was planned annually. In the morning students would attend a program and then board buses to an amusement park, Cedar Point, in Sandusky, Ohio. When it came time to go to the senior class trip, one student attended the program but started walking away from the school. I asked where he was going and inquired if he wanted to go on the trip.

The student did not have the funds for the trip. The teachers and I took up a quick offering to pay for the park admission and give him spending money. Each time I see him, he reminds me that I am the reason he graduated from high school. He didn't know that he is one of the reasons I stayed at the high school.

One day I was standing outside of the school, my ritual every morning, with my students.

An African American parent came up to me and said, "I want to see the principal!"

I asked, "What can I do for you?"

He looked at me. "No, I mean the principal!"

"Oh," I said, "you want a white principal."

He was embarrassed because he truly could not get over the fact that a black woman was the principal. Ironically when I got home that evening, this man was standing in my driveway. He wanted my husband to paint his car.

I exclaimed to my husband, "That's the man who thought I couldn't be the principal."

We had a great laugh that day, and I continued to refresh his memory of the incident—every time I saw him.

Because I taught in the same community, I often encountered former students who were now parents of my students. I was sitting in my office anticipating the arrival of a student who had been disruptive in his classroom.

I hollered out, "Billy, get in here!"

A grown man ran into my office. He was definitely not the person I had been waiting for.

I asked, "Who are you?"

"I'm Billy. You were my teacher." He had remembered my voice and came running.

On a separate occasion, a student developed some difficulties with his parents, so they had asked him to leave their home. He was of legal age and living with friends. When it came time for the prom, he had no way to pay for the activity. This was a chance of a lifetime to be of service to a child. His coach and I arranged to pay for his necessities to ensure he did not miss that special event. That included a tuxedo, flowers for his date, and prom tickets. It was important to me that he not miss one of the most memorable nights of his life.

Another young man found himself homeless. My concern was that he receive the things he needed. He was a very personable young man, as well as an excellent student and outstanding athlete. His coaches stepped in and provided living arrangements for him. The head coach went far beyond his assigned duties for his players, often without any sign of appreciation from parents. Top-ranking colleges sought out students from our school because of this man's diligent work. The young man alternated holidays with the coaches and a friend's family.

When he graduated from high school, members of the faculty and staff attended his party, which another family had graciously hosted. Upon graduation, the head coach made sure he had transportation to the college he had been accepted into and provided him with a cell phone and laptop.

When he came home from college, he contacted me, and we would often meet for lunch or breakfast, as time permitted. He is now a college graduate and works successfully in his chosen field. I am very proud of him and his accomplishments. He still calls from time to time and wants to know how his "Mom" is doing.

I tried to extend honor and respect to parents coming to the school. Parents usually come to the school once a problem occurs. They should always feel welcome within the facility. If a student were constantly misbehaving in a class, the mother or father was invited to attend surprise classroom visits to see what was happening for themselves.

On some occasions I asked parents to spend the entire day in the school and escort their child to his or her classes. That included eating in the cafeteria, courtesy of the principal. It only took one daylong visit for any child not to want his or her parent to walk the halls with him or her. If students were causing trouble in the hallways, I made it a point to be at their classroom door and escort them to the next period. Believe me, no one wants to be seen walking with the principal either!

Naturally over the years, a few parents were upset with the administration and school policy. One parent arrived at my office to tell me that I owed her money because I had taken away an open container of soda from her daughter the previous day. She said she had bought the drink for her daughter's breakfast. A full breakfast, free of charge for the majority of students, was served daily in the cafeteria. She was insistent and then refused to leave the building. This policy was in place as a safety measure for students. The security guard eventually escorted her out of the building.

A parent came into the office upset that her daughter's cell phone was stolen while in school. She arrived and demanded that my secretary get me immediately. It is not in my nature to be addressed or ordered about in that manner. Cell phones were not permitted in the school at the time and were considered contraband. The parent later apologized for the outburst. We continued to have cordial meetings from that point on.

Perhaps the most puzzling times were when parents wanted to argue about their children being tardy for school. The initial bell rang to allow students to go to their lockers and proceed to their first period class. By the second bell ten minutes later, all students were expected to be in their classrooms, seated, and prepared to begin class. This was not a homeroom period. It was an academic class. If a student was walking into the building or in the hallway when the second bell rang, he or she was obviously late.

Some wanted to challenge the clocks or give various excuses for the lateness instead of teaching their children to be on time. All students were excused the first three times they were late every semester. When severe weather or subzero temperature was a concern, the superintendent called for a two-hour delay to the start of school. The delayed admission to school was not held against the students. That meant the student could legitimately be late six times in 180 days.

There was also the day when two young men got into a fight after school. The Pennsylvania School Code specifically outlines the school's responsibility for students on the way to and from school. It is called the Port-to-Port (door-to-door) philosophy. One of the young men had made disparaging remarks to the other young man about his family. (The administration was not previously made aware of the comments.) As a result a fight broke out once they left the school building.

My assistant principal and I rushed to break it up. A call was made to each of the parents to explain what had happened and what the consequences of their actions would be before allowing the boys to go home. Parents were to bring in the boys for a conference the next morning. We made sure that they were transported safely to their homes. The parent of the boy who had started the fight insisted he not be given any form of discipline. This is yet another example where parents did not want any consequences for their child's negative behaviors.

In any school year and in any school district in the country, a bomb threat may be phoned into the school. Protocol must be strictly followed; precautions must be taken. Faculty, staff, and students are required to exit the building and wait in a designated area until the building is checked in its entirety. Special police with bomb-sniffing dogs are in charge until it is determined that there is no credible threat.

After one such bomb threat, I was listening to a talk radio station while driving to school. One of the parents phoned in, upset because the students had to wait outside in the sun for an extended period of time. He said it was too hot for students to be exposed to the heat. Obviously I called in to give my response, and I was immediately put on live radio.

It seemed the temperature was of greater concern to this parent than the welfare of the student body. What concerned me the most was the fact that some of these same students had gone to an amusement park a few days earlier when the sun was shining brightly, and nobody complained about the possibility of sunburn.

On one occasion several members of the faculty received intimidating email threats. The city police, administrators, IT personnel, and faculty were put on notice. The e-mails were later found to have been transmitted from a computer in the library of a nearby college. Upon further investigation, the suspect was identified and charged. He acquired the e-mail addresses from the faculty listings on the district's website and randomly chose his targets. When confronted in the courtroom, he had no clue who his victims were. Surprisingly enough I never got any e-mails.

Then there was the time that a student pulled the fire alarm while I was out of the building eating lunch. It was "Take Your Son/Daughter to Work Day." Usually I could not participate in this event because of my schedule, but I decided to bring Jonathan to school with me that day. I had not been gone long when I received a call. The waitress came over and handed me the phone.

When I asked how she knew me, she responded that she was told to look for the pretty, well-dressed lady. That I could take. I quickly returned to the school and found the fire trucks in front and the faculty, staff, and students outside. The student who had pulled the alarm was waiting in my office.

Once I came into the office, he fell to his knees and began to holler, "Jesus, Jesus, Jesus!"

I guess he thought that his prayer would change things!

On another occasion, I called the parent of a student who was standing outside the campus and making no effort to enter. I asked the mother why the student was not in school. Over the years I found I needed to carefully word my questions if I wanted to elicit the truth. She answered he was up in bed sleeping because he was sick that day. All the while I was looking at this young man standing on the sidewalk.

"Go and check on him," I requested.

Clearly I could hear her footsteps as she climbed the stairs and called his name. She returned to the phone and told me he was in bed sleeping. I told her to check the bed again because someone had apparently broken into her house and was sleeping in her son's bed. I could see him standing outside my window. Parents often make excuses for their children's behavior, and some outright lie for them.

Television reporters were outside of the building one morning, attempting to get feedback because of a situation that occurred. Choosing not to give a statement, I referred them to the superintendent's office for official comment. When I was watching the six o'clock news that evening, I noticed that the reporters had interviewed two of my students, and they had appeared on the news program.

Since I knew when the reporters were in place, I called the station to verify my suspicions. The next day I called the girls into my office. They had skipped classes and were caught because of the desire to be seen on TV.

There were numerous instances when I paid for SAT tests, postage for information needed for students to graduate, General Educational Development (GED) textbooks, college application fees, correspondence courses, and so forth. On one occasion a parent sent a note with her son, stating that she and her four children had no food. I called her to inquire and then contacted a friend who owned a grocery store. I made arrangements for the family to receive a fifty-dollar voucher to purchase food. The owner called me back after their shopping trip to inform me that the mother bought prime meats (steaks and roasts) and junk food. She then took out her own cash to buy cigarettes and lottery tickets.

Another time I sent a parent to the food bank to get additional groceries. She would not accept their donation because she said they weren't the brand names she was used to.

Often my beliefs were called into question. A parent told me his son should not face disciplinary consequences because he attended church. The son had used the Lord's name in vain after becoming very angry. I questioned if the boy had said "Amen" after his outburst.

"If he wasn't praying," I told the man, "he was cursing."

My secretary told me that I had a call waiting. The caller had asked for Sister Respress, a title used in many black churches. She wanted me to give her $500 to pay her electric bill. I had no idea who the woman was and refused her request. She told me I wasn't a Christian because I wouldn't give her any money.

At Christmas there was a coordinated effort to raise money to buy items for families in need. We contacted the parents for clothing and shoe sizes and a wish list of inexpensive items within our budget. Most families were grateful to be chosen. There were those few who were not. One woman asked for a pricey game system and things that could not possibly be purchased with our limited funds.

Another parent wouldn't come to the school to pick up the gifts. She wanted them delivered to her home. Once the packages arrived, she called out from her resting place on the sofa to come in. She never got up to acknowledge the presents or the students.

Another family that was homeless attended our church. The mother's situation really touched me. Our missionary society gathered personal articles that were needed. An invitation was extended for her family to eat Christmas dinner with my family. I had previously purchased coats and clothing for them.

Without notice the mother left town with a man she had recently met. She called to explain what had happened. I told her there was no need to give details. We all make choices in life and are responsible for the ones we make.

One of my students came to school every day in the same clothing. We had enacted a dress code, and he dressed according to the guidelines. His very dirty clothes looked as if they had never been washed. I wanted to give the student new clothes, but I was afraid that my gesture might offend his parents.

I called the father and told him that his son had won a competition in the school. His prize was five complete school uniforms, pants and shirts. He was overjoyed, and the student was thrilled to have new clothing. There was, of course, no contest, but it was a victory for the child. The student took pride in his appearance after that. His uniforms were kept clean.

Frequently all schools face dangerous situations. Early in my administrative career, a call was received from an upset parent who feared for the safety of her child. I was told that the father would arrive shortly. The police were notified, and the building was put on lockdown. He did come to the school, and the police subsequently stopped him. In his car was a loaded shotgun.

Fortunately students trusted me enough to provide valuable information regarding potential threats. A note was left on my desk one morning, stating a boy was in possession of a handgun. The day had not begun technically; the children were still eating breakfast in the cafeteria. I notified the proper authorities and went to the location to approach the student.

He had flashed the gun while riding on the bus that day and placed it in his backpack. I picked up his backpack, put it over my left shoulder, and embraced the boy with my right arm as we started walking out of the lunchroom.

I asked if he had a gun; he admitted he did. Because of God's providential care, no hurt or harm came to anyone that day. Ten years later he was convicted of murder and is now spending the remainder of his life in prison.

When the parent of another student died unexpectedly, the mother called from the hospital. She wanted me to break the news to her children. Of course I refused. That was no way for children to learn that a parent had passed away. Instead her children were transported to the hospital.

The mother contacted me a few days later. Her family had never made connection with a church in the community because they had only lived in New Castle for a short period of time. She had no one else to turn to. She asked if my husband would perform the funeral. He did, and the elders and musicians from our church assisted him.

I could recount more incidents that occurred during my career. My heart was broken on more than one occasion when I realized the pain that many students endured as they attempted to receive an education. Hopefully the love shown had a positive impact on the lives of the young people entrusted in my care. M. Scott Peck defines love as "the will to extend one's self for the purpose of nurturing one's own or another's spiritual growth. Love is as love does. Love is an act of will—namely, both an intention and an action. Will also implies choice. We do not have to love. We choose to love" (www.goodreads.com/quotes/150190-love-is).

Chapter 9:
MY EDUCATIONAL PHILOSOPHY

Student learning is the goal and people are the mechanisms for producing and sustaining student achievement.
—Gray and Streshly (2008, 15)

I am committed to the educability of all students. The guidelines of the Interstate School Leaders Licensure Consortium (1996) require that administrators ensure that students have the knowledge, skills, and values needed to become successful adults. That belief also entails a willingness to continuously examine one's own assumptions, beliefs, and practices. Shamefully there are schools and educational leaders across the United States that do not align themselves with this viewpoint wholeheartedly. There are also those districts so consumed with the results of standardized testing that they have forgotten the real reason for the existence of schools.

The call comes forth to "Raise the test scores!" But at what costs? School districts place excessive amounts of pressure on their existing staff, often lording over them the threat of replacement if the desired outcomes are not reached. As a result the morale of many teachers has descended to its lowest depths. It would not surprise me to find out that many suffer physical ailments as a consequence of extreme anxiety. If these conditions persist, I predict a flight of great teachers from the ranks of teaching positions across the nation.

Numerous studies have been conducted, citing factors that attempt to explain why our young people have not achieved their full potential in educational institutions, workplace, and society. The research frequently identifies poverty, environment, personal hardships, marginalization, and inferior education as a few explanations. Many more reasons could be added to this list. To this end there are persons in the educational community who have accepted the dire straits of our schools.

As a minority female who grew up in a lower economic stratum, I refute the negative assertions on children. Faith leads me to believe that students can be motivated when offered the appropriate learning environment, nurturing, training, and skills. It is incumbent on educators to have higher expectations while exacting clear-cut standards for student achievement. They have to raise the bar on their levels of expectancy. Mediocrity cannot be tolerated or accepted. Schools serve as the great equalizer for economically distressed children.

Thernstrom and Thernstrom (2003, 2) explain that literacy is a "gatekeeper, and the deadline for learning is alarmingly early. For many students ... the die is cast by eighth grade." According to a study by the US Department of Education, students who have not acquired an appropriate level of reading and math by eighth grade will probably never attain them by the end of high school.

Lisa Delpit, a leading researcher in urban classrooms and author of *Other People's Children*, implies in her work that we should not teach less content to poor, urban children, but rather teach more. She notes that people with power often see poor children through a "culturally clouded vision" (Delpit 1995, xiv). They often regard these students as "other" and "see damaged and dangerous caricatures of the vulnerable and impressionable beings before them" (Delpit 1995, xiii). She encourages educators to recognize and build on cultural strengths within children and maintains that a sense of family and caring in the schools must be created.

Negative perceptions of inner-city schools persist because the positive elements of these facilities are not celebrated. We hear and read about the setbacks, not the successes. I realized early in my professional career that children are children. There would be no need for a principal in any school if there were no difficulties. As the educational leader, I had to be forthright and direct when confronting both the positive and negative situations as they occurred. I took a strong stance on advocacy, discipline, and advancement. Creation of a nurturing atmosphere in the schools was cultivated by building positive relationships with students. I took time to both talk and listen to students.

In order to achieve some level of success, educators need to comprehend and appreciate the community, family dynamics, and culture of their students. This is crucial if relationships are to be forged. Culture (the entire way of life) includes religion, customs, traditions, and language. Once the effort is made to understand people, it is easier to interact and connect with those involved. These alliances lead to improved levels of communication. Oftentimes the lack of communication and/or miscommunication causes the most conundrums for educators.

To become as efficacious as possible, I developed a strategy of management using best practice research and combined approaches that fit my personal style of leadership. I could describe my methodology as "management by walking around." I came to believe that a principal's work priorities should include frequent stops into classrooms.

Gray and Streshley (2008, 110) reviewed studies conducted by Blasé (1985) and Blasé & Blasé (1986) that indicate a "principal's visibility in classrooms and placing curriculum and instruction at the top of school priorities are strongly linked to improved student discipline and acceptance of advice and criticism from teachers." They further suggest that the benefit of having a visible principal is realized greater by low-income and low-achieving students.

After a few years, I was promoted to the position of principal of the Ben Franklin Junior High School, the oldest junior high school still in existence in the United States at that time. Constructed in 1922, it was an impressive architectural structure. Superintendent Ben G. Graham created a new configuration for the division of grades. The junior high housed grades seven through nine and became the model for schools across the country. John Philip Sousa played at its opening.

Eventually the building was closed due to consolidation in the district. The combined junior/senior high school now accommodates grades seven through twelve.

God continued to prosper my career. In 2007 I was named principal of a combined New Castle Junior/Senior High School. Visibility and availability were among my priorities for leadership. The click of my heels down the hall meant I was on the move. Senior high schools have traditionally been run by men and generally not those of color. Because of my gender and race, I had to address certain attitudes from the onset of the appointment. Eleanor Roosevelt's quote, "No one can make you feel inferior without your consent," was proudly displayed on a plaque in my office and served as a daily stimulus for me (www.brainyquotes.com/quotes/authors/eleanor_roosevelt.html).

Being seen in the hallways and classrooms is the best advice I could give to aspiring administrators. Once the bell rang, all the principals in my building walked the halls. Teachers stood vigil by their doorways. Informal visits were made to individual classrooms as frequently as possible. There was no notification given to either faculty or students. Of course formal evaluations were held two times per year, as the state of Pennsylvania required. Walking into classrooms unannounced was a signal to students that they never knew when I would show up. That meant the teacher needed to be prepared in teaching and students needed to be actively engaged when I arrived.

Disobedience and disruptions in the classroom could not be tolerated because they hindered the academic progression of others. If I noticed someone not giving his or her full attention, I stationed myself next to that boy or girl. Suddenly the student became an adept listener and participated fully in the lesson. Later I would chat with the student and tell him or her that I appreciated his or her cooperation and would like for him or her to demonstrate that same enthusiasm for learning every period of every day.

On some occasions I would just come in and take a seat. I stayed no longer than five to ten minutes. A review of study guides that were being used and observations of teacher techniques were par for the course. Everyone was expected to be involved in the educational process. Positive elements of my experience were shared with the teachers once I saw them, and words of encouragement were given to reinforce their good work. Often a note of appreciation was sent to the teacher. The walk-through process was strongly influenced by the technique suggested in the Downey Walk-Through System (Downey 2004, 3–4), which focuses on professional growth. The walk-throughs promote a collaborative and reflective school culture. The system has five key elements:

(1) Short, focused, yet informal observations
(2) Possible areas for reflection noted
(3) Curriculum as well as instructional focus
(4) Follow-up feedback on occasion and not after every visit
(5) Informative and collaborative communication

If there were noticeable issues of class management, a formal visit was immediately scheduled for the classroom. Continued instances of the teacher's inability to supervise his or her classroom were addressed in post-observation conferences and upcoming ratings. Every opportunity was given to improve teacher practices and procedures. This process was intended to augment student learning and improve the learning environment of the classroom. I used Robert Marzano's *Classroom Management That Works* as my manual. At times the teachers would invite me to participate in the lesson. The history teachers knew my educational background and often asked for my input. I realized then that I truly missed teaching.

The visible presence of an administrator is vital. I strategically planned trips to the cafeteria. If I needed to retrieve a student for previous misbehaviors, the lunchroom would fall silent as I entered, each not knowing who I was coming for. I have been known to ride more than a few buses when students were disruptive. Imagine entering the bus and seeing your principal seated there. While en route, drivers in nearby automobiles would signal their approval with a thumbs-up or a honk of their car horns.

The focus of schools should always be the students. Everyone can be a winner in school, in my opinion, when given the appropriate incentive. I integrated the NASA slogan "Failure is NOT an Option" into the mission of the junior/senior high school. Those words were emblazoned on a banner, which still confronts all entering the building.

The message is taken from an alarming incident involving astronauts returning from space. In the spring of 1970, the Apollo 13 spaceship faced peril as it circled the moon. Many, including some working at NASA's ground control center, gave up hope that the crew and spacecraft would return safely to earth. The ground control became aware of the ship's inability to reach Earth with its current power supply.

After much discussion and many possible solutions voiced, the director of operations, Gene Kranz, became adamant about the fate of the astronauts. He said, "We never lost a man in space, and we're sure as hell not going to do so on my watch. Failure is not an option" (Blankstein 2004, 1–2).

This is the same approach I adopted as an administrator: to lead by example and never let failure be considered a choice. Our children are too precious to allow them to be unsuccessful in life. We can never be satisfied as long as failure looms over future generations and is accepted by those who could have made a difference.

I regard teaching as my mission and my calling. Remembering my perceptions of my high school days made me determined not to replicate them with my students. All students can learn, but students learn in different ways. Students are entitled to an equal opportunity to success, irrespective of what they have been handed by virtue of birth. Many parents move out of urban settings because they believe the suburbs provide a better education for their children. It is what I term as "economic segregation."

In my travels and conversations with other principals, I have found that all schools—large or small, urban or suburban, rich or poor, or predominantly black or white—have their own share of difficulties and disruptions. The acquisition of certain complications comes with the territory. The apostle Paul wrote in his First Epistle to the Corinthians, "When I was a child, I spoke as a child, I understood as a child, I thought as a child, but when I became a man I put away childish things" (1 Cor. 13:11).

Do not be alarmed when children act like children and need supervision and guidance in their daily routine. Students may willfully violate existing guidelines and discipline codes. Whitaker (2012, 8) contends "it is the people, not the programs that determine the quality of a school."

In correlation with my educational philosophy, I amalgamated my thoughts into what I consider to be the ABCs of Education.

A = ACADEMIC EXCELLENCE AND ACCOUNTABILITY

The goal of academic excellence should be extended to every student while requiring accountability from our educators. In every state and community in the United States, school culpability is a theme that is commonly heard and discussed. This premise has led parents, policy-makers, and community leaders to demand improvements in students' achievement levels. The focus is on higher teacher standards and enhanced student performance.

The question remains, "How can this be achieved?"

Whitaker (2012, 109) states, "Great teachers keep standardized testing in perspective. The focus is on the real issue of student learning. Talented teachers make a difference in the learning process and impact their students' possibilities for success."

Every student is someone's child. I cautioned teachers under my watch to treat the children in their classrooms as if they were their own. What does that mean? You want your own to succeed. Provide teaching strategies to ensure that others succeed. You want your children to be treated with respect. Respect those children in your classroom. Teach as if there were a parent sitting in the classroom every period of the day. Collins (2001) contends that leaders need "a dedication to making anything they touched the best it could possibly be" (Gray and Streshly 2008, 5).

Teachers who exhibit a passion for teaching will most likely pass on that enthusiasm to their students. High expectations should be evidenced in the work of both teachers and students. Whitaker (2012, 34) states, "Great teachers have high expectations for students but even higher expectations for themselves. Poor teachers have high expectations for students but much lower expectations for themselves."

Given the proper motivation, students will rise to the expectations that their teachers and schools set. I believe that students want to be challenged daily to work hard and set goals. By expanding student horizons, an implicit message is revealed, "I have faith in you." Often students recognize that their teachers do not expect anything but mediocre academic performance from them.

I met a man once who, at the time, served in a management position on a college campus. His vocabulary was impeccable, and he clearly was highly educated. He shared with me that he spent his early school years in special education, primarily because of his disruptive behavior. After several years and many teachers who treated him as if he could not achieve, he realized his potential and began to study the dictionary to enhance his knowledge. He also began to comport himself in a more positive way. Soon he was transferred into regular classes and later given a college-bound schedule. He decided to change and took the steps necessary for success to occur.

I believe, if you have positive expectations for those in your charge, the students will most likely respond with positive results. Sometimes the students themselves develop the positive expectations and take the initiative to ensure a better life for themselves.

Educators must mentor and furnish positive experiences for struggling students. Blankstein (2004, 98) notes that schools may sometimes provide "the only bastion of stability in a student's life." In my opinion the element of care must be incorporated into the educational formula to enhance our children's guaranteed success. Schorr (1988) reinforces the potency of schools in stating, "When acting in concert to create a reclaiming environment and to build systems to prevent failure, school communities dramatically enhance the likelihood for student success" (Blankstein 2004, 98).

The impact of effective teachers can be impressive. When educators recognize that what occurs in the classrooms does matter and embrace the philosophy that all children have the ability to perform at accelerated levels, schools across the land will undergo improvement. Stronge (2007, 32–33) asserts that "factors affecting student achievement such as poverty, parent participation in schooling, nutrition, and a host of others are viewed as obstacles to overcome, not obstacles that are insurmountable."

Sometimes educational leaders must assert their professional authority in order for both parents and students to recognize the benefits of accelerated coursework. A mother approached me once and said her daughter did not want to take the college-level courses that had been suggested because they were too hard and required too much study time. The parent confessed that the student was too busy enjoying other hobbies, like talking on the cell phone.

I told the mother, "Let your child choose her flavor of ice cream when she goes to Dairy Queen, and let us choose her courses for high school."

Children have to be challenged to achieve their full potential. My father taught me that anything worth having is worth working for. Life does not come easy. That young lady now enjoys a successful professional career. Those accelerated classes prepared her mind for study and enabled her to receive college credits for courses taken in high school.

Our son Jonathan was told that he could attend the college of his choice for his intended major, biomedical engineering. We would attempt to pay for his education as best we could because we did not want him to be strapped with staggering student loans throughout his life. At one point he applied for a local scholarship and was denied. I was later appointed to that same scholarship committee and asked what had happened with my son. He would be attending a private college, which came with higher tuition. That seemed to be an even greater motive to award money to a student.

A fellow committee member told me I should have made him go to a cheaper college. I should note that he did have several offers to pay his full tuition if he chose to attend those universities. He was accepted to every college and university that he applied to. I left it up to him, and he chose The Johns Hopkins University.

The sacrifices made to send him to Baltimore proved invaluable for his future. As parents we will probably never have a great deal of money to leave to our children when we are gone. What we can do though is invest in their education. That investment can help bring lifetime security. The pedagogy, once they own it, can never be taken away. He worked hard during those years. Many high schools do not fully prepare students for the demands of these prestigious institutions.

He recently told me that he was often discouraged by people concerning his career choices. I wish I had that knowledge back then. I certainly would have addressed those statements face-to-face. He did graduate nevertheless, and Baylor College of Medicine in Houston, Texas, recruited him for further study. Funding was provided for him to continue his schooling. He earned a PhD in molecular physiology and biophysics/cardiovascular sciences in 2012 and is now working in an area of innovative medical research.

Much pressure is put on schools to perform. National educational legislation requires accountability for student learning. Schools have no choice but to adjust teaching strategies and include differentiated learning styles in the delivery of information. Tucker and Stronge (2005, 1) note, "We know intuitively that these highly effective teachers can have an enriching effect on the daily lives of children and their lifelong educational career aspirations. We now know empirically that effective teachers also have a direct influence in enhancing student learning."

Researchers have determined that the teacher is the most important factor that shapes student learning. Whitaker (2012, 7) reminds us that "teachers are a school's keystone of greatness. There are really two ways to improve a school significantly—get better teachers, and improve the current teachers."

B = BEHAVIOR

The inclusion of behavioral guidelines refers to discipline in the classroom and the management of conduct on the part of both students and teachers. When teaching on the college level and as principal, I advised teachers that they were teachers twenty-four hours a day, in my opinion. Teachers must model professional behavior at all times. That means educators have to be cautious about postings on social media and public conduct. How can you correct a student for inappropriate language if you are swearing in front of them or publicizing profanity on your Facebook page?

As witnessed in many recent news reports, teachers are held accountable for unacceptable activities when posted on the web and often suffer repercussions for their actions. In my experience, I have found that students do not mind correction when done in the proper manner. Teachers were encouraged to develop appropriate relationships with parents and students.

Blankstein (2004) suggests the gap between school and community can be closed by employing the following principles in the development of positive family relationships:

- building mutual understanding and empathy
- effective involvement of family and community
- reaching out to family and community (169)

Parents provide a much-needed support system. Phone calls and notes to parents are generally appreciated. With the advent of e-mail and online informative programs used by most school systems, keeping in touch is even that much easier. They give access to current materials being presented in classrooms. Use of such programs allows parents to review the results of quizzes, tests, and homework assignments. They offer direct communication with the teacher. The first time I received a progress report from my son's high school, I was nervous about opening it. In my experience, progress reports were always written in the negative, sent to the struggling or failing student. This report was comprised of all positive remarks. From that time on, I encouraged teachers to do likewise.

Discipline issues are commonplace in schools today. Quite often school disruption comes from those who have given up hope of trying to learn anything and seek attention from the teacher, even if it is negative. Pupils cannot learn if the classroom is noisy and filled with distractions. The stage for student learning relies significantly on the teacher's ability to manage his or her classroom.

What I found to be a severe disruption when I began my teaching career in the 1970s seems hardly worth mentioning today. A pupil threw a paper wad at my student teacher when I stepped out of the classroom. That behavior is a minor transgression today when compared to the weapons violations, cell phone complications, bomb threats, bullying, cyberbullying, sexting, absenteeism, fighting, and drugs that have infiltrated America's schools.

Having a clear plan of consequences always worked for me. As a teacher I included students in the creation of simple classroom rules focused on the concept of respect.

As a principal the policies were approved by the board of school directors and within the confines of the Pennsylvania School Code. It was important that I was fair and consistent when complying with the guidelines. Influential members of the community sometimes questioned the interpretation of the discipline code. Consequences were administered with equity, no matter who the students were and regardless of their social standing, even if the students were relatives of mine. I was not always the most popular administrator because of this conviction. Discipline codes are reviewed annually and amended as new infractions arise.

When I was in elementary school, every day began with prayer and a scripture reading, followed by the Pledge of Allegiance to the flag. There were no fears of attending school back then or thoughts of shootings and murders on the campus. Schools were considered safe havens for all. When prayer and Bible reading were forced out of the building, the evils of society marched in. Security systems and officers must now protect schools to ensure a measure of safety for those in attendance.

In 2010 a colleague and I developed an evening program for at-risk students to continue their education in a nontraditional setting. The term "at-risk" has been used in a number of forums. For me it signified those that were, because of any number of circumstances, in jeopardy of not completing high school and/or dropping out of school. Reasons why students do not graduate include a failure to attend school regularly, incarceration, teenage pregnancy, serious health issues, domestic violence, a move from place to place, learning disabilities, low test scores, and disciplinary problems. Often these young people simply do not want to get up early enough to attend school in its traditional time frame and instead choose to be absent from school.

This at-risk program provided a setting for students who misbehaved or earned their way into alternative education because of breaches to the attendance and/or behavior policies. Those decisions ultimately impacted their ability to graduate. Students who had previously not functioned well under conventional school conditions were now given the opportunity to have their schooling provided from three thirty until eight o'clock in the evening. Attendees were only permitted on school property during scheduled class times. They were also not allowed to go to school activities such as dances, basketball games, and football games during their stay. Participation in these events was considered a privilege, not a right. Classes were assigned by junior or senior high grade level with only certified teachers in the classrooms. Physical education was mandatory, and each student's schedule included a counseling component. Guest speakers from the community provided thought-provoking presentations to students.

Transportation was provided; the school district furnished meals. Placement in the alternative education program was for a minimum of forty-five school days. The return into the daytime schedule was contingent on the fulfillment of the attendance and academic goals established upon entering the program.

A graduation ceremony was held at the end of their stay, complete with a certificate of hard work and a cake. Parents were invited, and pictures were taken of the families. For some that ceremony was perhaps the first true sign of a recognized accomplishment. Many students asked to remain in the program because they realized success in school. The ultimate goal was to develop a climate that was conducive to scholastic growth.

As a principal I was considered a strict disciplinarian. That firmness was tempered with love. Sometimes I would hand a copy of the school discipline code to those in my office for official reprimand. Students were well acquainted with the policies because they were reviewed numerous times throughout the year, posted throughout the building, and included on the district's website. Both parents and students attended orientation sessions to cover school policy. The New Castle Student Handbook, which was carried daily, also contained the entire set of guidelines. I would often question students who violated the school discipline code.

I would sometimes ask, "Tell me what the code says that your consequence should be."

One student said, "I would suspend me."

I had to wait until he left the room to shake my head about his response.

C = COLLABORATION

Author Roland Barth (2001, 60) noted, "I wonder how many children's lives might be saved if we educators disclosed what we know to each other." A collaborative culture focused on teaching and learning is central to this ideology and results in high-achieving schools. That means that educators discuss our defeats and celebrate our victories with one another. Why not take advantage of best practices that produce favorable outcomes?

Killion (2011, 14) states that "collaboration among educators builds shared responsibility and improves student learning." She insists that students benefit the most when teachers pool their knowledge. The team strategy is best accomplished when the collaboration is done on a daily basis or as often as possible.

Gray and Streshly (2008) encourage the formation of professional learning communities. They encourage the following guidelines to achieve this goal:

- provide opportunities for staff to play a significant role in goal setting, problem solving, and making decisions that affect their work
- encourage openness in others
- facilitate effective communication
- encourage teacher involvement, eliminating issues of risk and threats
- shift thinking from a focus on teaching to a focus on learning (111)

The principal is the educational leader of the school. I always considered myself a "teacher of teachers." In that stead, I felt it my duty to practice sound educational principles. The collaboration efforts should not end with the sound of the bell that ends the day. To build a strong educational base, schools must connect with families and community members on all levels while responding to diverse community concerns and needs. This includes being cognizant of community resources and utilizing them to their maximum potential.

Chapter 10:
THE CONCLUSION OF THE MATTER

Let us hear the conclusion of the whole matter: Fear God, and keep his commandments: for this is the whole duty of man.
—Ecclesiastes 12: 13

My mother enjoyed many years of independent living while residing in our home. When she needed additional care, I elected to retire from my position as principal of New Castle Junior/Senior High School. The decision was difficult to make. History had been made with my appointment to this post. My love for the children and school was obvious. The faculty and staff were like family. Through times of disappointment and frustration in the school district, a rainbow of hope was still revealed at the end of each storm. I had spent thirty-six years of my life investing into the lives of others.

In retiring from the school system, I also left my part-time teaching position at Butler County Community College. Truthfully I was not sure what I would do with my time. After all there is only so much *Law & Order* a person can watch.

Mother's health issues were such that she was unable to care for herself. She had been self-reliant during those early years. She and her best friend, Mrs. Emma Taylor, would plan and attend events such as lunches, plays, and movies. Although older than my mother, Mrs. Taylor was the driver. My mother would try to copilot from the passenger side. It was a hilarious sight to behold. She would also schedule rides to doctor appointments through the senior citizen agency. She loved to get her hair and nails done. Her beautician would often take her to lunch and drive her home. When she was unable to go out to receive these services, the stylist and technician came to my home. Unbeknownst to me, she even had her eyebrows waxed. She still wanted to look good in her nineties.

My sister Kathy drove from New Haven when my mother took a turn for the worse. I called the hospice nurse, and she quickly came to the house. My brother and his wife, Eva, arrived from Pittsburgh. Truthfully we thought Mother was going to die at any moment. We were in agony. The nurse didn't give us much hope either. I called another of her close friends to come. People heard about her condition and poured in to see her. The next morning I went into her room, and she was alert and asked me when I was going to have her nails done again. God is good!

I was the child that stayed in or near my hometown and continued to care for my parents. The House of Prayer was always my church, and I had never joined another congregation since its inception. It was my father's baby, and I wanted to see it grow and flourish. When others walked away, I stayed. It was my home away from home, my lifeline to my God. There was no sacrifice too great to ensure I attended every pastoral anniversary given my father.

One year I was admitted to the emergency room of St. Elizabeth Hospital after having a reaction to new medicine. After the intravenous tubes were disconnected and I was discharged, I rushed to Sampson Street to be in attendance.

The farthest I lived from my parents was approximately twenty miles in Youngstown, Ohio. If they called, I came in a hurry. One particular evening as I was facilitating a meeting at the vocational school, my father's brother came into the room. He was looking for me because Dad had gotten sick and needed emergency surgery. Because of my close proximity, I immediately went to the hospital and was with him for the procedure. My siblings had all moved at various times to locations across the country. If my parents needed me, I was available. They probably didn't realize that I needed them as much as they needed me.

My retirement came as a new chapter of my life. For over a third of a century, I got up early in the morning and took care of my various duties. My workday was long and often included supervision of athletic and social activities. I spent many evenings away from home. I never understood all the complexities and calls of football and basketball games, but I watched intently and acted like I did. I thoroughly enjoyed eating the popcorn there too.

My time for studying was usually four o'clock in the morning. The house was peaceful and my thinking process was at its best. Once I retired I spent most of my days tending to my mother. There were occasions when I spent the entire night sitting beside her in a chair. Sometimes I was unable to attend Sunday church services because she did not feel well enough to accompany me.

I had spent much of my life in education. It seemed as if I were wasting my expertise if I did not actively engage in teaching or supervision. After her death I intended to increase the amount of time working with the church and develop programs within it. Those hours spent preparing to teach Bible study or learning new songs for choir practice were precious. I loved singing and directing the choir. I made faces at the members if they hit a bad note. Since they were facing the audience, they couldn't laugh, but everyone could see their shoulders moving. They sang with joy and appreciated the ministry of music. I filled in as the teacher of the adult class in Sunday school and soon found myself teaching full time. Studying energized me and renewed my mind.

My husband began to develop chronic health issues. We drove rather than flew to see our son in Texas because we had obtained a dog. Our shih tzu-poo was too big to fit under the seat of a plane, and I refused to have her put in the luggage area. We made the twenty-four-hour drive two or three times a year. Normally we drove about eight hours a day and stayed overnight at a pet-friendly hotel.

At one point blood clots developed in my husband's leg. Although he was treated for the condition and he found some relief, we found it to be a reoccurring affliction. During one of our trips to Texas, he was taken to the emergency room in the Houston Medical Center and advised that he could not drive or fly anytime soon. I returned home because we could not stay away from the church for such an extended period of time. He was the pastor after all.

As a result I stepped in for him and preached the Sunday morning message for nineteen weeks in a row. I suggested a title for his sermon when he resumed preaching, "Let Your Setback Be Your Comeback." He never used it. (I guess he thought I was trying to be funny.)

The bouts with blood clots continued. One afternoon he went to his physician for an appointment but could hardly make it home. A special test had been done in the office, and the doctor called when he received the results. Torrance was told not to drive and to call an ambulance if I were unable to bring him to the hospital. He was admitted, and the doctor feared damage to his heart.

I stayed at the hospital until about nine o'clock and went home to rest. A call from the nurses' station was received within the hour, requesting my return. He had been transferred to the ICU. His specialist was called in. Those were some very intense moments as the hospital staff continued to work on him. Eventually he responded to the treatment.

A serious dialogue began about the possibility of moving to Texas. We had previously talked about relocating, but it was like a distant dream. My husband's brother, Albert, and his wife, Angel, lived in nearby San Antonio. I say nearby, but it is really a three-and-a-half-hour trip. Nothing in Texas is close. One changes total perception of distance after sitting in rush hour traffic for more than an hour to go twenty miles. We anticipated living closer to them and seeing each other more often. The church, friends, and few family members were the ties holding us to our hometown. They were the strong connections that linked us to western Pennsylvania.

We decided to purchase a home. Jonathan continued the search in our absence. We prayed about the church, the one that my father had founded. As a charter member, I had worshipped there for more than fifty years. Even when I lived in Youngstown, I made the journey on Sundays and Tuesdays. When I was in undergraduate school, I came home on Sundays, frequently bringing other college students with me. They were always eager to accompany me because my mother would prepare a soul food dinner for my guests and me. That also meant I could spend time with my family and throw a few dirty clothes in the washer as a bonus.

We decided the move would be good for both of our health. There is something about seeing sunshine most days of the year that makes arthritis not show up to aggravate a person. Jonathan knew exactly what to look for in a house. During previous trips to Texas, we toured model homes and compared notes on the features we liked. The initial plan was to build, but our home sold so quickly that we needed an alternative plan. Our son called and said he found the house. It was recently built and had been occupied for only a brief period.

According to the story I heard, the former owners needed a larger yard so their newly acquired rescue dog could have more room to run. Thank God for the dogs in our lives! Sight unseen, we sent the money to hold it! We trusted God's and our son's judgment. We flew in to look over the house and found it to be just what we were looking for. It hit all the items on our wish list. My husband wanted a three-car garage and a sprinkler system. The house contained both. We desired a single-story home. No more stairs for us! The gated community included a recreation center and a pool. There were walking trails throughout. The yard was just big enough for Torrance to plant a garden and tend to the lawn. I didn't want him to overwork himself outside. The house also had a lakeside view.

It immediately felt like home. This was another testament as to how God works. He gives us our needs and throws in our wants as an added plus. We purchased it and prepared to become Texans.

Our last Sunday at the House of Prayer was the celebration of the pastor's anniversary, an annual event held on the second Sunday of March to commemorate the date that my husband became pastor. This observance would additionally be deemed as our farewell service. Mixed emotions filled us. I stared at my parents' picture hanging prominently on the wall. A picture of my husband and myself was affixed next to theirs. As I looked over the church, memories flashed before my eyes. It never occurred to me that I would ever leave.

My husband was clearly torn, as I was, because we had put so much of our time, sweat equity, and tears into cultivating the ministry. As pastor he had bought the building and completely remodeled its sanctuary and basement. The purchase of several city lots during his tenure added to the existing property. The structure was enlarged by fifty feet. He also constructed a baptismal pool, replaced old classrooms in the basement with a social hall, hand-built an altar in the front of the church, and bought new chandeliers, seating, and lectern. Torrance primarily did the manual labor.

I remember what the old church looked like. Used theatre seats that often left marks on the back of people's clothes filled the sanctuary. There was no air-conditioning, but somehow we never noticed the heat. (A few hand fans were available for those who did.) The floor tiles were coming loose, and dust filled the room when the shouting started. The area for worship had been long and narrow but cozy. The building had great acoustics, and the music sounded wonderful. A detailed hand painting of the three crosses on Calvary covered the entire back wall of the small pulpit.

In my mind I could envision my father standing on the platform, pouring out his heart. Because the building had previously been rented, there were no guarantees if a great deal of money were poured into renovations. Now the building was beautifully decorated and comfortable because it belonged to the members of the House of Prayer. In my opinion it was one of the most attractive churches in the area.

Many pastors had words on that special day. Most, if not all, were given a time to address my husband about the strides he had made and his impact on the community. They commended him for his commitment to the church. One speaker stood out among them. My brother Israel told my husband that God said he was released from this ministry. A flood of tears flowed when the confirmation came from God that it was all right to move forward in our lives. Our church members were visibly shaken. There was not a dry eye in the house.

The church meant everything to us. It was my connection to my childhood and comprised of people who truly loved me. The members lightened the load of caring for my parents. The House of Prayer had been such a great part of our lives. We both knew that my husband's health could not take the strain of preaching. His preaching was very charismatic. By the time he was done, his clothes were soaking wet from perspiration. He would often be nearly hoarse by the end of the sermon. It was how he delivered the Word. The decision to move was the right one to make, and now it was the correct time to execute our plan.

I found a personal meaning in Hebrews 11:1, "Now faith is the substance of things hoped for; the evidence of things not seen." Wishing to complete an education, I earned degrees through grace, hard work, and study. After praying for spiritual maturity, I found the pathway to growth in the deep-seated roots of my father's teachings. Hoping to make a difference in the lives of people, I incorporated stewardship into my commitment to the church, school, and community. Desiring to teach at a college, I waited for the invitation to present itself. It was nearly thirty-five years in the making, but it came nevertheless. Longing to live a full life and see my grandchildren born was a petition I placed before God. Two of my sisters had died at early ages, one at thirty-one and the other at forty-two. Secretly I questioned God if longevity were in my plan. God granted me the gift of life. In the near future, I will be eligible to collect Social Security benefits. I consider myself to be blessed and highly favored of God.

Faith directed me, corrected me, fortified me, and protected me. It helped me recognize that God ordered my footsteps. He worked out all the difficulties faced, answered many of the questions raised, and loved me unconditionally in spite of my inadequacies. My father, the Reverend Israel L. Gaither, steered me into my faith walk, but my desire to be stronger in the Lord equipped me as I journeyed. I continue to be thankful for *My Father's Faith*.

Epilogue

The good teacher makes the poor student good, and the good superior. When our students fail, we, as teachers, too, have failed.
—Marva Collins (Howe 2003, 85)

Andy Hargreaves and Michael Fullan (Howe 2003, 5) define what education and schooling means to them in *What's Worth Fighting for Out There*. "Among the many purposes of schooling, four stand out to us as having special moral value: to love and care, to serve, to have power and, of course, to learn." This statement of belief summarizes the primary roles of educators. It remains the duty of the learning communities to retain and uphold these standards for our most precious commodity, our students, are at stake. If we lose the children to illiteracy and neglect, the nation is at risk. The upcoming generations will serve our military, head our businesses, discover new medicines, seek previously elusive cures, preserve democracy, protect our rights, teach our progeny, and lead our nation. It is a massive undertaking.

The time spent preparing *My Father's Faith* has renewed my vigor and restored by energy. I have depended on my faith in God throughout my life and career. I trust God fully for my future. I consider the fundamental teachings of my childhood to have enhanced my walk with God. I encourage anyone who is discouraged or currently enduring a period of defeat to look to God for the remedy. Be persistent in your quest for the designs that God has in store for you. Hold fast to your dreams for they will come to fruition as God manifests the promises He has made in His Word. He cannot lie.

I still believe in our children with my whole heart. I have an unquenchable fire of hope still burning. Nothing can stop the children of God from obtaining their aspirations. I urge the church, educational community, and secular community to continue to bind together to fulfill the prophetic destiny that is set before us. The Lord has great things in store for His people! I want to live to witness all His blessings pour down on us. I advise those who are charged with the great task of educating our youth to not take that calling lightly. There may be many difficult days in responding to your mission, but the victory comes in knowing that lives have been positively touched by your care and concern.

My years spent working with the church, community, and educational arena have proven to be sources of solace. I would hope that I left those areas a little better than when I started. I was destined to care for my parents as they aged, as well as the children of my sisters who passed away. As I look back over my life, I am content in the knowledge that I gave all I had to ensure the well-being of my family.

The passages of *My Father's Faith* are intended to stimulate the faith process in others by reviewing my father's life and his influence on my own. I have explored scriptures as they relate to the day-to-day struggles faced. In doing so, my life has become transparent as I revealed many of the difficulties that have been faced along the way. I count each and every curve as a learning situation and grew from the disappointments and tragedies that I endured.

The philosophical foundation of my educational beliefs has also been unveiled. The years of working with students have blessed me beyond measure. I value the many people who poured their wisdom into my life and molded my thinking. I continue to walk in my faith.

REFLECTIONS FROM MY DAUGHTER

Famous songwriter, acoustic master, and lyricist India Arie wrote a song, "Strength, Courage and Wisdom." When I heard that you were undertaking this exciting endeavor, this title came to mind. These are the three words I would use to describe the attributes needed to take on a solo project that comes from the heart. It takes a great deal of strength to revisit memories involving lost loved ones. Courage is key when one steps out on faith to share her story with the world! Wisdom is something you shared with the city of New Castle, Pennsylvania. You have gone above and beyond to give yourself to your community, church, and family, never asking for anything in return except for the expectation for those around you to give their best and strive for success. You have truly been an inspiration in my life to continuously strive to achieve and never become content or complacent with mediocrity. I am extremely proud of you as a professional woman of color, a great spiritual leader, and, most of all, my mother. Congratulations on your endeavor, and thank you for paying homage to my grandfather.

Akilah Eshe Daniels

REMARKS FROM MY SON

First, I want to acknowledge this great accomplishment. I admire you greatly. To write a book is not an easy task. The writing process took creativity, motivation, and, most of all, accountability. This story will bring a piece of history to the public, affirm the memory of a great man, and provide spiritual inspiration to the masses. Your life and work deserves to be noticed. It deserves to be noticed because of your belief in the words of Dr. Martin Luther King and refusal to accept that the bank of education is bankrupt. You refused to believe that there are insufficient funds in the great vaults of opportunity in this nation. You provided our city's youth with the opportunities of this nation, not just our small town. Some have pondered the question "When will she be satisfied and give up?" The answer is "Never." You were never satisfied as long as there were still victims of illiteracy. You did not rest until all children realized the importance of an education. The city of New Castle will be forever in your debt.

Second, I would like to acknowledge you for being a wonderful mother. You have always been there for our family and were always willing to sacrifice for our needs. You helped me see and understand God's will for my life, a plan I could not accomplish alone. As I walked, you pledged to march with me from primary to graduate school and even in fatherhood. I often pause to think about it. You have always been there at my side and on my side, from the moment I drew my first breath. I remember distinct memories from my childhood in which you demanded greatness, a quality that made me who I am today. How do I fully appreciate the woman whose perseverance, love, and example shaped me into who I am? I can't possibly thank you enough or do you justice in this message, but one day I hope to contribute to your life in a meaningful manner as you have mine. Thank you. I love you.

Dr. Jonathan Lee Respress

WORDS WRITTEN AND PRESENTED TO ME BY MY FRIEND MRS. MICHELE MCBURNEY

Into your family
a child was given.
She was brought,
unstamped and untarnished,
into your care.
Your arms will hold her close,
comfort her,
guide her through the years.
Your hands will brush away the tears,
inspire dreams,
lead her into the future.
Your action will inspire her,
pave her path,
usher her into a future.
In return,
she will give you joy,
laughter,
and, most of all, love.

References

Banks, Cherry. 2000. *Gender and Race as Factors in Educational Leadership and Administration*. San Francisco: Jossey-Bass.
Barth, Roland. 2001. *Learning by Heart*. San Francisco: Jossey-Bass.
Blankstein, Alan. 2004. *Failure Is Not an Option*. Thousand Oaks, CA: Corwin Crown Press.
Bynum, Shirley. 2003. *An Awesome Force: Black Spiritual Women as Powerful Resources in the Education of Poor Students*. Unpublished doctoral diss., University of North Carolina, Greensboro.
Carlson, Dennis. 1998. *Power/Knowledge/Pedagogy: The Meaning of Democratic Education in Unsettling Times*. Boulder, CO: Westview Press.
Casey, Kathleen. 1993. *I Answer with My Life: Life Histories of Women Teachers Working for Social Change*. New York: Routledge.
Collins, Patricia Hill. 1998. *Fighting Words: Black Women and the Search for Justice*. Minneapolis: University of Minnesota Press.
Dantley, Michael. 2005a. "African American Spirituality and Cornel West's Notion of Prophetic Pragmatism: Restructuring Educational Leadership in American Urban Schools." *Educational Administration Quarterly* 41: 651–74.
———. 2005b. "The Power of Spirituality to Act and Reform." *Journal of School Leadership* 15: 500–19.
Delpit, Lisa. 1995. *Other People's Children*. New York: The New Press.
Downey, Steffy, Frase English, and William Poston. 2004. *The Three-Minute Classroom Walk-Through*. Thousand Oaks, CA: Corwin Press.

Dunbar, Paul Laurence. 1913. *The Complete Poems of Paul Laurence Dunbar*. New York:

Dodd, Mead, and Company.

Florence, Namulundah. 1998. *bel hooks' Engaged Pedagogy: A Transgressive Education for Critical Consciousness*. Westport, CT: Bergin & Garvey.

Foster, Michele. 1997. *Black Teachers on Teaching*. New York: the New Press.

Freire, Paulo. 1970. *Pedagogy of the Oppressed*. New York: the Continuum International Publishing Group, Inc.

Gariepy, Henry. 2006. *Israel L. Gaither: Man with a Mission*. Alexandria, VA: the Salvation Army.

Garner, Rochelle. 2002. *Contesting the Terrain of the Ivory Tower: A Study Examining the Spiritual Leadership of African-American Women in the Academy*. Ann Arbor, MI: UMI Dissertation Services.

Gates, Henry. 1987. *Figures in Black: Words, Signs, and the Racial Self*. New York: Oxford Press.

Gay, Geneva. 2000. *Culturally Responsive Teaching: Theory, Research, and Practice*. New York: Teachers College Press.

Gray, Susan, and William Streshly. 2008. *From Good Schools to Great Schools: What Their Principals Do Well*. Thousand Oaks, CA: Corwin Press.

Greenberg, Jon, Linda Qiu, Katie Sanders, and Derek Tsang. 2014. "Fact-Checking Claims about Race After Ferguson Shooting." www.poynter.org/news/mediawire/266133/fact-checking-claim-about-race-after-ferguson

Hine, Darlene, and Kathleen Thompson. 1998. *A Shining Thread of Hope: The History of Black Women in America*. New York: Broadway Books.

hooks, bel. 2003. *Teaching Community: A Pedagogy of Hope*. New York: Routledge.

———. 1994. *Teaching to Transgress: Education as the Practice of Freedom*. New York: Routledge.

Howe, Randy, ed. 2003. *The Quotable Teacher*. Guilford, CT: the Lyons Press.

Hull, Gloria. 2001. *Soul Talk: The New Spirituality of African American Women.* Rochester, VT: Inner Traditions, International.

Hull, Scott, and Barbara Smith, eds. 1982. *All the Women Are White, All the Blacks Are Men, But Some of Us Are Brave.* New York: the Feminist Press.

Killion, Joellen. 2011. "A Bold Move Forward." *Journal of Staff Development* 32: 10–14.

Ladson-Billings, Gloria. 1994. *The Dreamkeepers: Successful Teachers of African American Children.* San Francisco: Jossey-Bass.

Lerner, Michael. 2000. *Spirit Matters.* Charlottesville, VA: Hampton Roads Publishing Company, Inc.

Liebert, Elizabeth, and Andrew Dreitcher. 1995. *The Spirituality of the Teacher.* www.theway.org.uk/back/s084Dreiter.pdf

Lincoln, C. Eric, and Lawrence Mamiya. 1990. *The Black Church in the African American Experience.* Durham: Duke University Press.

Merriam-Webster Dictionary. Retrieved on January 20, 2015. http://www.merriam-webster.com/dictionary.

Painter, Nell. 2006. *Creating Black Americans.* Oxford: University Press.

Palmer, Parker. 2000. *Let Your Life Speak: Listening for the Voice of Vocation.* San Francisco: Jossey-Bass.

———. 1998. *The Courage to Teach.* San Francisco: Jossey-Bass.

———. 1993. *To Know as We Are Known: Education as a Spiritual Journey.* San Francisco: Harper.

Rodgers, Harrell R., Jr. 1996. *Poor Women, Poor Children, American Poverty in the 1990s.* Armonk, New York: Sharpe Publishing.

Rhodes, Ron. 2011. *1001 Unforgettable Quotes About God, Faith, and the Bible.* Eugene, Oregon: Harvest Publishers.

Rosenman, Samuel, ed. 1938. *The Public Papers of Franklin D. Roosevelt.* New York: Random House.

Stewart, Carlyle. 1997. *Soul Survivors: An African American Spirituality.* Louisville: Westminster John Knox Press.

Stronge, James. 2007. *Qualities of Effective Teachers.* Alexandria, VA: ASCD.

The Holy Bible: King James Version. 1970. Nashville: Thomas Nelson Publishing.

The Holy Bible: New International Version. www.biblegateway.com.

The Jossey-Bass Reader on Educational Leadership. 2000. San Francisco: Jossey-Bass, Inc.

Thernstrom, Abigail, and Stephan Thernstrom. 2003. *No Excuses: Closing the Racial Gap in Learning.* New York: Simon & Schuster.

Thurston, Anne. 1995. *Because of Her Testimony.* New York: the Crossroad Publishing Co.

Tucker, Pamela, and James Stronge. 2005. *Linking Teacher Evaluation and Student Learning.* Alexandria, VA: ASCD.

Vespa, Lewis, and Rose Kreider. 2013. *America's Families and Living Arrangements: 2012.* www.census.gov/prod/2013pubs/pdf.

Wade-Gales, Gloria, ed. 1995. *My Soul Is a Witness: An African American Woman's Spirituality.* Boston: Beacon Press.

Walker, Alice. 1983. *In Search of Our Mother's Garden.* Orlando: Harcourt & Brace & Co.

West, Cornel. 1994. *Race Matters.* Philadelphia: the Westminster Press.

———. 1999. *The Cornel West Reader.* New York: Civitas Books.

Wiersbe, Warren. 1982. *Be Successful.* Colorado Springs: David C. Cook.

Whitaker, Todd. 2012. *What Great Teachers Do Differently: 17 Things That Mean the Most.* New York: Routledge.

Williams, Delores. 1993. *Sisters in the Wilderness: The Challenge of Womanist God-talk.* New York: Orbis Books.

About the Author

Dr. Jacqueline M. Gaither Respress is a recognized educator and administrator in eastern Ohio and western Pennsylvania. She is considered an effective leader and a sought-after inspirational speaker in both religious and secular circles. Her faith in God, experiences as an educator, and conclusions of educational research have been combined in the formation of this work. *My Father's Faith* recounts her journey through life, one greatly influenced by the Christian faith instilled in her as a child.

Dr. Respress earned a Bachelor of Science in Education from Slippery Rock State College, a Master of Education from Youngstown State University, as well as a Doctorate in Education from Youngstown State University. She is certified as both a principal and superintendent by the Pennsylvania Department of Education.

In 2014 Dr. Respress became the recipient of Youngstown State University's Diversity Leadership Recognition Award for Community Leadership. Slippery Rock University previously designated her as one of their Women of Distinction, and she was also selected as one of Lawrence County's Outstanding Educators. She coauthored the alternative educational program The Academy and facilitated its operations for at-risk students in her school district. The creation of the motivational project Children of Promise highlights her efforts to witness student achievement. The initiative targets students of color to reach academic success in high school and at the postsecondary level.

Her talents have not been limited to the classroom. She served as the first lady and choir director of the House of Prayer Church of God in Christ and educational coordinator on both the local and district levels. Dr. Respress became the first female and first African American to serve as principal of the Ben Franklin Junior High School and an amalgamated New Castle Junior/Senior High School in the district's 150-year history.

Often described by many positive qualities, she notes that "woman of God" remains her favorite. She has been married to the Reverend Torrance Respress for thirty-three years and currently resides outside of Houston, Texas. She is the mother of Akilah and Jonathan and stepmother of Darrick, Marcus, and Anthony.

Printed in the United States
By Bookmasters